THE GAME OF THEIR LIVES

Voices of the Football People

DERICK ALLSOP

MAINSTREAM
PUBLISHING
EDINBURGH AND LONDON

First published in Great Britain in 1995 by
MAINSTREAM PUBLISHING COMPANY (EDINBURGH) LTD
7 Albany Street
Edinburgh EH1 3UG

ISBN 1 85158 800 0

A catalogue record for this book is available from the British Library

Typeset in Janson by Saxon Graphics Ltd

Printed and bound in Great Britain by Butler & Tanner Ltd, Frome

CONTENTS

Contents

ACKNOWLEDGEMENTS

I would like to thank the many who have kindly given their time, their thoughts, their co-operation or helped, in whatever way, the compilation of this book. Some I will doubtless overlook. To those, my apologies, also. The others are: Tim Crabbe, Gordon Taylor, Neil Midgley, Mike Walker, Graham Kelly, Eric Hall, Bryan Robson, Dave Bassett, Alan Green, Jürgen Klinsmann, Gary Bennett, Tim Flowers, Terry Venables, Canon JR Smith, Ron Atkinson, Gordon Strachan, Mick Brown, David Meek, Alex Ferguson, Alan Ball, Andy Gray, Roger Dilkes, Paul Brownlow, Mary Smith, Gwen Blockley, Roy Frisby, Chris and Donna Siddon, Chesterfield Supporters' Club, Nicola Bellamy, Chesterfield FC, Graham and Ann Turner, David Davies, the FA, the Football League, *The Independent, The Sunday Telegraph*, Jane Nottage, Ray Matts, David Smith, Steve Acteson, David Lovett, Sue, Natalie and Kate Allsop. The pages of *Rothmans Football Yearbook* and *Guinness Soccer Who's Who* have, as always, provided invaluable information.

INTRODUCTION

T he glory game is gone, the beautiful game banished, we are told. It is now branded the game of sleaze and shame, dope and dopes. We hear of thugs on the pitch, thugs off the pitch; whingers instead of wingers; a maelstrom of hatred, abuse, anger and recrimination. No, it is not the perfect football world, but then is it not a mite naive to expect it to be? Was this not also hailed 'the people's game' long, long ago? As such it must surely represent the full gamut of human emotions and traits. How can the world of football be so different from the real world beyond when people provide the bridge?

A sense of perspective, rather than rampant hysteria, is called for here. For all the dirges of despair, gates and ratings have continued to go up, the allure of the game and the loyalty of the masses defying the cynics. The vast majority take the view we still have a game to celebrate and to exalt. They are as weary and contemptuous of the peddlars in doom as they are of the lunatic fringe.

Be it the opium of the people, a spiritual calling or a wonderful irrelevance, this is their game and remains precious to them. Millions structure their lives around their football and their clubs, whether big or small, famous or anonymous. For the very lucky the game is also their livelihood. For all it is a source of passion, fulfilment, frustration, bravado and endless debate.

This book seeks to capture the compulsion that has endured against the backdrop of an often turbulent and controversial, yet always engrossing and ultimately dramatic, English season through the voices of football people. From across the spectrum of the game, from players, managers, administrators, referees, media and fans, we hear of the personal and collective appeal that has made football the games of their lives. From:

Tim Crabbe, chairman of the Football Supporters' Association . . .
'If there's one group of people within football who care more than anything else about the future of their clubs it's football fans. The fan is the number one sponsor of football.'

Introduction

Gordon Taylor, chief executive of the Professional Footballers' Association . . . 'I have a job to try and create as many jobs as possible, and I am a great believer in a game that, a few seasons ago, saw Wrexham, the 92nd club, beat Arsenal, the top club, in the FA Cup.'

Neil Midgley, former FIFA referee, now FA match observer and League match assessor ... 'Refereeing is a subject that will always have us hot under the collar, and that is its beauty as well as its beastly bit. I do believe that's part of the fun for people watching football. We'll never be seen to get it perfectly right.'

Mike Walker, manager of Everton, January to November 1994 . . . 'Any top manager will tell you it's a 24-hour-a-day, seven-days-a-week job. Football is almost more important than family. It's marginal. You've got to have the enthusiasm as well as the ability. You can have some of the greatest players, but if they don't want to know, no chance.'

Graham Kelly, chief executive of the Football Association . . . 'I always say that if there is an issue to be faced, let's face it, let's look the criticism in the eye and discuss the issue honestly and openly – if it's agents in football, or it's alleged bribery, or if it's drug-taking or whatever it is.'

Eric Hall, agent . . . 'My concern is not what the public or journalists, or even chairmen, up to a point, think about Eric Hall. It's the players. Eric Hall is good at his job, for the players.'

Bryan Robson, player-manager of Middlesbrough . . . 'Of course I'm conscious of the comparison with Keegan because everybody mentions it all the time. He's done a great job at Newcastle, but that's Newcastle. I just blinker myself here and if I can improve this club on half the scale Keegan's done at Newcastle, then I'll be delighted.'

Dave Bassett, manager of Sheffield United . . . 'It may well be that I'm a bit Joe Blunt and say what I feel and sometimes say the wrong thing ... It might frighten one or two people that I might not be quite the IMAGE, I might not be the polished article, as they say, but the one thing I think I am is up front, I'm honest, I admit that I make mistakes.'

Alan Green, BBC radio commentator . . . 'I don't mind making an ass of myself. I think people listening like that. They like you to be human ... They like the personal thing. Lots of people I work with don't like it ... I am exactly the same off air as I am on it. I am the same opinionated, far too opinionated, Irishman.'

Jürgen Klinsmann, formerly of Tottenham Hotspur and Germany . . . 'I have learned so many things since I started playing. Probably when I stop playing I will look back and say, "It doesn't matter if you scored 20 or 30 goals a season, but that you learned different languages, you knew how to handle different mentalities. This is something you can be proud of."'

Gary Bennett, formerly of Wrexham . . . 'After all I'd had to put up with it was nice to know people saw something else in me. People were beginning to respect me for my football and my goals. Let's face it, goals get you more respect in this game than anything else.'

Tim Flowers, of Blackburn Rovers and England . . . 'I'd like to be able to look in the mirror when I'm 40, and hopefully still playing, and say, "Tim, you've done everything you possibly could to be as good as you possibly could." If I can do that I'll be happy. If ever I thought I'd not . . . I would resent myself for it.'

Terry Venables, England coach . . . 'I'm not going on holiday with players. I'm looking for success and if I favour someone it's normally because I think he's a better player. That's the only favour I've given and will continue to give.'

Canon JR Smith, vice-chairman of Bury . . . 'A lot of things have happened that don't really bring joy to people who love football, and the great thing is that football is for everyone . . . I don't have any problems reconciling the church with football. If I can go to football I'm happy to go.'

Introduction

Ron Atkinson, manager of Coventry City . . . 'I've never played politics in football . . . What annoys me is that certain things have been done by certain people at the Villa to discredit me, and I know full well what's going on.'

Gordon Strachan, player-coach of Coventry City . . . 'There are a lot of good people in the game and that is why, the longer I am in it, the longer I want to stay in it. The people are good, I like their sense of humour, and they are honest . . . 99.9 per cent of them are.'

David Meek, football reporter . . . 'The new pressure came in more of a free-for-all, cut-throat tabloid situation. It's less scrupulous now mainly, I think, because newspapers see themselves as having to compete with television, as entertainers. Straight stories are being confined to fewer papers, while more popular tabloids are tending to make more of a circus out of stuff.'

Alex Ferguson, manager of Manchester United . . . 'It makes me laugh when people go on about the so-called incidents our players have been involved in this past year and you see some of the tackles that go on in other games. There's not been one broken nose, broken jaw, gash, knee ligament injury or even a bled wart, not a flippin' thing, as a result of our players' tackles.'

Alan Ball, manager of Southampton . . . 'When the phone call came with the offer to manage a Premier League club, all the questions came flooding back: "Can you do it? Do you think you're good enough? Can you hack it, son? This is your chance. If you don't make a good job of this you'll go down in history as not a bad player, yes, someone who's brought kids up, the Darren Andertons of this world, yeah, you could do that, but you couldn't manage a top side."'

Andy Gray, Sky television commentator . . . 'We've listened to the public, given them what they want and given football a platform it's never had. And we've given it financial backing it's never had. And yes, if you like, we have given the BBC and ITV a kick up the backside.'

Roger Dilkes, referee . . . 'You get the odd call, the odd letter ... You hear on the grapevine about your colleagues getting stick and various things . . . But I think the attitude of referees is that they prefer just to get on with the next game and after a couple of weeks it's gone. Time is a great healer.'

Mary Smith, Chesterfield supporter, whose 35-year-old son is also a Chesterfield supporter and is wheelchair-bound . . . 'Football is a release for me because it has been hard, especially since my husband died . . . I'm looking forward to Wembley . . . I think they can win down there this time, too. Besides, we want them to go up so we can go to some different grounds.'

Ann Turner, wife of Graham, manager . . . 'I don't think you realise what a different person you can be until you have a break from it . . . You can enjoy normal things in life like going on a shopping trip, of spontaneous laughter on a Saturday morning. I think it's our fault, as a family. We've made him bring it home. We've shared everything . . . Now when jobs come up the kids tell me not to look at the atlas to see where we might be living.'

Graham Turner . . . 'The game does involve a lot of heartache one way or another for all the family but it is worth it. We played at Wembley in the Sherpa Van Trophy final . . . The crowd was in excess of 80,000 and Andrew was the mascot, and whatever the heartaches and the problems, moments like that are priceless. That's why you put up with it and still want it.'

CHAPTER 1

In the Name of the Fan

Tim Crabbe, chairman of the Football Supporters' Association

The voice of the fan was once restricted to tribal chants, explosions of exultation and cries of despair: the atmospheric sounds that were taken for granted not only by those who ran our game and our clubs but also by the supporters themselves. Then the voice began to articulate the fans' cause, to express rights and demands, and the authorities began to listen. In the wake of the disasters at Heysel, Bradford and Hillsborough, they had to. The new standing of the football fan (the other, older standing of the fan is something we shall come to) is as momentous a feature of the modern game in this country as the advent of splendid stadia with perfectly manicured pitches and acceptable spectator facilities.

Football supporters still have their gripes, notably regarding the removal of terracing, the restrictions on travelling fans and anomalies in admission prices. But at least the voice is heard and recognised as a voice of reason rather than the anthem of a hooligan movement. Enlightened administrators and sponsors acknowledge that the fan, whether through the turnstile or at the souvenir shop, remains the game's most important investor.

The Football Supporters' Association exists to ensure the voice of the fan is never again lost in the wind of dictatorial or bureaucratic rhetoric. This body seeks not to rule football but to enhance it for all those who care about the old game. That mission has been led, since June, 1994, by Tim Crabbe, a 29-year-old Crystal Palace fan who lives in Manchester and works as an academic researcher at the city's university.

'The Association sprung up in 1985, really in the aftermath of Heysel. The initial hotbed of the Association came out of Liverpool and the negative image that was coming over about football supporters in general at that time. A group of fans wanted to challenge that notion, put over a better image of football fans and try to provide a voice for the millions of decent fans out there.

'Then, in the aftermath of Hillsborough, there were important issues for supporters to get across to the authorities, such as the campaign against the ID card scheme, and certainly in attempting to address questions about safety and have some input into the Taylor Report, which followed the Hillsborough disaster.

'There were a large number of issues around that time that supporters' voices needed to articulate, and that provided a focus for the FSA's work in the early years. I don't think it could come through the old supporters' club system because there was a feeling they had become closely entwined with the structure of the football clubs, in terms of providing a service which augmented what the clubs themselves were about – organising away travel, social functions and what have you at the clubs. While that close relationship between the supporters' clubs and the football clubs is not necessarily a bad thing, there's also a need for an independent voice. There are always possibilities of supporters coming into conflict with the football authorities, both at national level and club level, and maybe some of the traditional supporters' clubs are not best equipped to get over the supporters' concerns where the fans do fall out with the institutions.

'The organisation is open to all football supporters provided they go along with the terms of the Association. There are certain things we wouldn't put up with, such as racist attitudes or sexist attitudes. It's about people who support football rather than any particular club. People tend to join on the back of a national campaign, others because of a club-based concern, such as we have seen at Manchester City, QPR and Tottenham.'

Membership – for a fee of £10, or £7 if you are young, old or unemployed – is up to around 3,000 and as well as the 'feel good' factor you will receive a regular magazine, be invited to 'something like a comedy event' (no doubt there are plenty of fixture suggestions for that) and the opportunity to join an organised trip to an Italian Serie A match.

'We are also looking at more ambitious services,' Crabbe says, 'such as a legal advice service where supporters who have come into trouble with the law, like the Manchester United fans in Galatasaray, require help.

'Initially Rogan Taylor was the FSA. He provided a wonderful voice for the media and the association came over as a large and vibrant organisation because of the effectiveness of the media work, but not a lot happened to build the base. Rogan invested five years of his time as chair of the FSA and it can be quite an arduous task when it's something you're not getting paid for. I think most of the chairs have tended to feel that after a couple of years it's time to let new blood come through and that will probably be the same with me.

'The job can take up as much as 20 hours a week and that can put a strain on things at home. My partner is from Birkenhead, Merseyside. She despises football. I suppose she would have a soft spot for Tranmere but she doesn't understand what this football malarkey is all about. Perhaps if we build up a stronger FSA organisation we might be able to employ full-time staff and provide a permanent office base.

'The football supporter is listened to far more in the modern age than, say, pre-Hillsborough, and I think the FSA can claim a lot of the credit for that process having taken place. The Premier League recognises they need to speak to fans and has established Premier supporter panels, with a lot of input from us.

'We have played our part in making clubs much more aware of the fans. Just basic things like toilet facilities, etc, are improving. I think it's coming over that we're not a bunch of radical football fans trying to take control in a political fashion. It's actually about good business practice. The bottom line for a decent and successful company like Marks and Spencer is care for the consumer, and in football the fan is the consumer. Sometimes in the past that has not been recognised, forcing unnecessary antagonism.

'If there's one group of people within football who care more than anything else about the future of their clubs it's football fans. The fan is the number one sponsor of football. We see the enormous amounts of money Manchester United declare as profits and hear less than 50 per cent actually comes through the gate. That can be misleading because without the fans you can kiss goodbye to all the merchandising.'

Crabbe has embarked upon a research project on racism in football – 'particularly focusing on some of the reasons that may prevent black fans from attending matches in the same proportion that black players are attracted to the game. I think there is a perception within black communities that football is racist, and a football environment can certainly be intimidating for newcomers. It's a question of breaking through, in the same way that black players broke through.

'A big bone of contention for fans up and down the country is treatment of away supporters, and the advent of all-seater stadiums. I'm personally not in favour of all-seater stadiums. That's not to say I want a return to archaic, crumbling terraces. I certainly want to see safe, comfortable stadiums. But I also want people to recognise that football stadiums are there for one purpose, and that is so the supporters can watch, and I think the supporters should decide how they go about doing that.

'There are a lot of people who are delighted with the introduction of seats and are very comfortable in them, and that is fine. But I would like to see the retention, within every ground, of an area of terracing: preservation, if you like, of the popular end, where people don't need a seat number to be with their friends. Such areas would continue to generate the kind of atmosphere the Jürgen Klinsmanns and Eric Cantonas say is so special about English football. Part of that came out of the terrace culture – the chants and the banter.

'We can look for 101 reasons why hooliganism might have developed within football, and it's not necessarily something that went on on the terraces. We've seen many incidents where seats and cushions off seats have been thrown. There were certain hooligans who had the attitude: "We sit here because we're that little bit more special than the plebs on the terraces."

'With the move towards all-seater stadiums there has been a dramatic reduction in the number of tickets available to away supporters. Indeed, at Maine Road, while re-building work has been going on, no away supporters have been admitted. I think the combination of creating all-seater stadiums and the removal of away fans is having a thoroughly detrimental effect on the atmosphere within stadiums. Where there's no group shouting for the opposition there's less inclination to get behind your own team, so the atmosphere becomes rather sanitised.

'Where away supporters are allowed they are quite often finding they are getting charged higher prices than the home supporters for similar facilities. Sometimes they find the adult prices are the same but that there are no concessionary prices. There are many instances where away supporters are being exploited. The away fan can spend something like £100 a week following his side, and not only that, he spends the rest of the week at work telling his mates about it. So he's also the marketing man for football. That fan needs to be protected rather than pushed away with the message "We don't want you in the new football era".'

But does the fan in the modern era get value for money? 'In certain instances he does but in others he doesn't,' Crabbe says. 'An awful lot of money has been injected into the sport, so the people in power recognise they do have a very desirable product which is marketable in areas that were never realised before. And television has been the main provider of that income.

'Palace introduced a pricing structure, with category A and category B matches, while they had limited capacity. It was £20 for the cheapest category A ticket and £16 for the cheapest category B. The early matches against Liverpool and Leeds were both category A, but while there was a full house for Liverpool there were only 13,000 people for the Leeds match. The price structure had some impact and surely it's better to get bums on seats.

'I went to Aston Villa around that time, had a good seat and a good view, and paid £12. I thought that was damn good value. I felt the facilities were better than at Crystal Palace, that I had a better view than I had at Palace, and yet I spent something like 40 per cent less for the ticket. If Villa can do it, Palace should be able to do it.'

But then football is not like any other form of entertainment. It's an involvement, a commitment, sometimes even more. 'I would agree with that entirely,' concedes Crabbe. 'Football is an integral part of my life. In many ways it reflects life. In 90 minutes of football you can experience every emotion of a lifetime: despair, joy, frustration, jealousy, everything. Maybe the person who goes to opera gets that out of opera, but I wouldn't.

'So when you get people who are particularly passionate about something then, yes, they are prepared to pay whatever price it is. That is part of the problem. The clubs know that. They know the regular fans, those who are hooked, will keep coming back. And it's the same with the money fans have to fork out for shirts and what have you. Man United fans are going to keep buying the latest United shirt. If the quality of the shirt is not as good as Man City's, the United fan is not going to buy a City shirt. There is a potential to exploit fans and some clubs are on the boundaries of doing that. We are trying to keep it in check.'

The quality of the domestic game, he acknowledges, has improved. 'I think whereas three or four years ago you were looking at the side winning the League being the meanest side, since then there has been a movement towards the top teams playing good, open football. Manchester United, Newcastle, Blackburn – sides with talented players, these were the ones dominating.'

Another bone of contention within the game has been the influx of foreign players. Crabbe says: 'I absolutely welcome the Klinsmanns and the Cantonas. There are those who suggest it's basically wrong to be drawing on foreign talent when there is talent in this country, but I think that at the highest level players like Cantona and Klinsmann add something that doesn't exist in our game, and they maybe bring out the best in our players. And I think you can also look further down the Leagues. Swindon, for instance, have had an outstanding contribution from Jan-Aage Fjortoft. Sure, there may be better players in this country than Fjortoft, but are Swindon in a position to get their hands on them?

'That brings us to another aspect – we've got to start asking about the transfer fees in this country. Take Chris Sutton. He's a good player and I'm sure he'll do well and play for England. But £5 million for him when Klinsmann can be bought for £2 million? Klinsmann is a proven World Cup player, he's set the English scene alight, and that was good business.'

Here, Crabbe has a bone to pick with Gordon Taylor, the chief executive of the Professional Footballers' Association. 'As I understand it, the PFA acted as the "agent" in Sutton's deal with Blackburn, negotiating on his behalf. If the PFA is prepared to accept such transfer deals then I think they have got to understand that people are going to look abroad. You can still get good deals abroad.

'I think one of Gordon Taylor's concerns is that we'll see the deterioration of the national team, as we saw in cricket. I don't think that will necessarily happen. If you look at the Italian situation:

probably the strongest league in the world and any great foreign player is immediately snapped up and taken there. Yet Italy got to the final of the last World Cup while we didn't even make it to the United States.

'Foreign players can open our eyes to how the game is played abroad. We often talk about the problem we have at international level being our insularity and the fact we can't appreciate other styles of play. Well, one way of getting some experience of international styles is to get some of it feeding into our game.'

Crabbe, like all football fans, has his views because the game matters to him. He believes the fan deserves to be heard and has a valid contribution to make.

'It's not about people trying to cause trouble or trying to be awkward, it's about something that people feel very passionately and they don't want to be pushed to the margins. They don't have to be there at the heart of the decision-making process, but they want to be kept informed, they want to be consulted. They want to feel the club cares about them in the same way they care about the club.'

CHAPTER 2

Brothers in Arms

Gordon Taylor, chief executive of the Professional Footballers' Association

A smart, mock-Georgian building near St Peter's Square, Manchester; security personnel and polished brass plates; a spacious, beautifully furnished main office. This is the home of the players' union today and a monument to the stature attained by its members. The pictures hanging on the walls of the office pay homage to the movement's pioneers and the squat, middle-aged man who works here conducts a tour into the past like a doting grandson.

Billy Meredith, the original Welsh wizard, a player with Manchester City and United, and a founder of the union, retains a special place of honour here. So does the story of the day he lay sick and destitute, beneath his bed an old suitcase containing his caps and medals. He told Cliff Lloyd, then secretary of the union: 'Always remind your members that those caps and medals didn't look after me in my old age.'

But then such characters and anecdotes, cherished though they may be, belong to another age. The union was born in 1907; it is 34 years since the historic abolition of the maximum wage. Players now have celebrity status and celebrity income; they play in magnificent, all-seater stadia with executive boxes and restaurants. Surely the players' union is an irrelevance in the modern game?

As a bobbing forward and now chief executive of the Professional Footballers' Association, Gordon Taylor has learned to cope with the uncompromising challenge. 'The union is more valid than ever, in all walks of life,' he counters. 'Of course there have been problems and patchy years. Arthur Scargill and the coalminers didn't always give unions the best of names, to the extent that even within the Labour Party there are reservations, despite the fact that vast amounts of their support comes from the unions.

'But you're looking to improve standards, you're looking to improve insurance benefits for members who have an eight-year career, you're looking to re-training for the future, you're looking to have a hardship fund for those who go by the wayside, you're looking to have pensions so that your money's best protected and you're not ripped off or exploited. And it's not just for the lower division players. The top players don't necessarily have financial advisors. We found top stars were more vulnerable than anyone, and when you have former players of the likes of Tony Currie out of work, broken marriage and let down in business, you have one of the very good reasons why we are taking positive measures for the benefit of the industry as a whole and developing a number of Government schemes.

'In '83 we developed the youth training scheme, and whereas before that you had about 200 boys a year joining clubs, we took advantage of that scheme to the extent that we now have 1,250 lads joining the game on a two-year basis, which is really the research and development side of the game.

'We had World Cup euphoria in 1994, but there was no UK side involved and clubs are looking for ready-made foreign players instead of looking to their own youth systems or the lower division clubs, which have traditionally been the breeding grounds. We feel the youth training scheme is really important because we should be bringing on our own talent. A survey of Premier League clubs showed that 50 per cent of the clubs had no more than two players in the team who had been brought through the ranks. Sixty-five per cent came from the lower division clubs.

'Despite the recession, the Taylor Report, the rebuilding of stadiums and reduced capacity, attendances have been on the up for eight years. No matter that hooliganism is being defeated, that increase is testimony to the quality on the pitch. The irony is that with the quality of the domestic product, with the great infrastructure we've got – 2,000 full-time players, 1,250 in youth training, more full-time clubs than anywhere else – we are not doing as well as we should internationally.

'Three years after the youth training scheme came the community programme. Players would go into schools, coaching, they'd get pensioners to clubs and tea dances, reducing that alienation between locals and clubs. They'd work with ethnic minorities and contribute to the curbing of hooliganism.

'Since that time, with six clubs, we now have well over 90, some non-League, some county FAs. It's creating work for the likes of Tony Currie, in Sheffield, Brian Hall, at Liverpool, and so on. We employ about 80 former players. With our television money following the introduction of the Premier League we've got £1 million back, half a million to the community programme to help clubs with their wages for the community officers.'

Let us return to the present players and the union. 'Every professional player is a member,' says Taylor. 'Everybody's in because benefits far outweigh costs, which are subsidised anyway. They have a non-contributory cash benefit scheme, five per cent of every transfer fee going into a central pot, which gives every player on retirement a tax-free cash lump sum, based on his years in the game and his average earnings.

'Then they have legal advice, grants for education, any course from coaching to deep-sea diving and a commercial pilot's course. And, of course, there's the accident insurance. Any player forced to retire is covered for at least six months of his contract, plus £5,000. We also have a special scheme where they can pay to insure themselves. We do, after all, lose about 50 players a year.'

Taylor, born in Ashton-under-Lyne, in 1944, played with 'all the Bs' – Bolton, Birmingham, Blackburn and Bury – and had a twilight spell with Vancouver in North American soccer, relishing the opportunity to rub shoulders with Pele, Beckenbauer and Carlos Alberto. He was chairman of the union before succeeding Lloyd as secretary in 1981 and has since become one of the most respected and consulted figures in the game, his sphere of influence extending far beyond the immediate welfare of his players.

His general concern for the health of the game is genuine, but then he recognises that all aspects will eventually affect the well-being of his members. His political acumen is razor-sharp, his campaigning zeal indefatigable. His opposition to the Premier League and any easing of restrictions on the signing of foreign players reflect paternal instincts. He cares for his flock, preferring to house them in a long tried and trusted League system. And when clubs have been endangered, he has fought on their behalf. He is equally proud of the Association's support to campaigns against hooliganism and racial prejudice, and the movement for better relations with supporters.

We must, though, return to this thorny issue of foreign players. 'We are far from xenophobic,' he pleads. 'I am, after all, president of the European Players' Association so I am aware football is a world game, but we need to be careful if we are to succeed internationally. Of course the Republic of Ireland, and Norway, with a number of English-based players, reached the World Cup, but then they weren't all that successful. I don't think any of the semi-finalists had a player from the English game. Remember Real Madrid had a tremendous side, with lads like Puskas, of Hungary, and Di Stefano, from Argentina, but Spain weren't too successful.

'It's a question of where you draw the line. The players voted Cantona Player of the Year. I must admit I couldn't see him as Fergie's type of player but he's been the icing on the cake at United. I have nothing against Cantona. I have nothing against any footballer in the world, but I have a job to do and football countries throughout the world, on average, say no more than three foreign players per team.

'Now you might say, "Why worry, Gordon, because the lads who have come in have done a great job?" In actual fact, £20 million went out of our game, abroad, in the summer of 1994. Since 1978, following Tottenham's purchase of Ossie Ardiles and Ricky Villa, there must have been hundreds of foreign signings and the vast majority have just not made the grade. That's sad. We don't want to see players exploited. Some say clubs should be able to buy as cheaply as they want from anywhere in the world, but if this process continues it's the lowest common denominator.

'Sir John Hall, at Newcastle, says he should be able to buy wherever he wants but it is not his job to look after the long term interests of English football. He might also consider the contribution of his English lads, like Peter Beardsley, who originally came from Carlisle, and Andy Cole, who didn't make the grade at Arsenal but did at Bristol City.

'Last year's transfer turnover was £19 million, £13 million profit going to the lower divisions. I don't know whether that sort of profit will be possible with clubs going abroad. Bear in mind also that the Premier League is getting about £80 million of football's turnover, compared with about £20 million divided by the rest of the League clubs.

'The fact is that most foreign players coming here are not better. Of course there are some fine exceptions, such as Ardiles, Muhren, Thijssen, Cantona, of course, Schmeichel, and then perhaps Klinsmann. We get stick but Hottiger got approval by us and tell me how many people are going to pay money and travel a distance to see him. I find it astonishing that people say the PFA shouldn't be like this and that our players will improve through playing with foreigners.

'One magazine suggested that a trialist would be better just by watching Klinsmann. It's like saying I'll be a better ballet dancer if I see Nureyev every week, or that every ballet dancer who danced with him became a better dancer. Tell me if it's logical for that to apply or if it isn't even a danger. There's no certainty that players who played with Pele or Finney or Matthews were better players. If anything, their teams suffered without them because they were reliant on them. I hope Barmby and Anderton do well because of Klinsmann, but I wonder. It's fair to say United are more polished as a team with Cantona, but whether the others become better players is another question.'

Taylor points out that 400 of his members were released on free transfers last year and maintains his Association is not responsible for pushing up transfer fees. But how about his involvement in the record £5 million move by Chris Sutton? 'We were involved only as far as wages were concerned. We looked after Sutton as we looked after Vinny Samways and David Batty. People come to us instead of an agent because so many players have been ripped off. We have a financial management company in the Midlands that looks after pensions and investments and employs people like Des Bremner and Bob Hatton, former players who are paid a wage and charge an hourly rate if it's a hands-on approach. No way did we organise the transfer fee for Chris Sutton.

'The Sutton deal was a special case, where you had a lad of a young age with tremendous potential. He's hopefully going to have another 14 or 15 years in the game, whereas Klinsmann is a lot older. But it was almost as if United, Everton, Tottenham and Arsenal were in there to push up the fee, like an auction house, to make sure that if Blackburn were going to get him they were going to have to pay absolute top whack.

'But that is a very inflationary figure and if others follow suit it is a worry. It concerns me in the way the £1 million fee for Trevor Francis, in 1978, concerned me because suddenly you have other clubs trying to compete, paying money they've not got. It would be churlish to criticise Jack Walker when the game should be grateful for such benefactors. But £5 million for an uncapped player? It could cause a spiral that sucks clubs in. As in the past, with Wolves, Swansea and Middlesbrough, it could leave clubs in peril. It's dangerous accounting and could, of course, encourage clubs to go abroad.

'If you find money is going abroad and not to the lower divisions, there's no justification for keeping the transfer fee system in being. If it doesn't help to create clubs and jobs there's every reason to say well, let's remove it. Eventually the lower division clubs would go out of existence and there would be no justification for keeping a youth system.

'I have a job to try and create as many jobs as possible, and I am a great believer in a game that, a few seasons ago, saw Wrexham, the 92nd club, beat Arsenal, the top club, in the FA Cup. If, indeed, the game contracts, we'll lose clubs, we'll lose players and a competition like the FA Cup will lose the glory.'

He does, however, see changes for the better: 'Out of the tragedies has come good. We've had to deal with hooliganism, we've improved grounds and safety. I felt it was an anachronism to say fans wanted to be shepherded, that it was cosy, standing up together. In this day and age, you've got to be looking to treating people as decent human beings, not cattle.

'The mood of supporters is so important to football. What most impressed me at the World Cup in America, in New York and Orlando, was how the supporters of Ireland, Mexico, Norway and Italy mixed after the matches, showing the game can be a vehicle for the finest ideals of sport. It was a reminder that we must continue to beat hooliganism, because it nearly caused the game's downfall in this country. America showed that the buzz the spectators get is as vital to the game as what's on the pitch.

'The game won't succeed in the future if it doesn't have that integration of supporters and the buzz they generate. The sponsorships the game has now, particularly from television and big commercial companies, will move on like butterflies if hooliganism returns or the stands are empty. The spectators put far more into the game than any other sponsor, well over £100 million a year in gate receipts. They are the lifeblood.

'Hopefully we can ensure away fans pay the same price as home fans. I can understand how the supporters sometimes feel isolated. I feel that as a players' organisation we have more in common with the supporters than with managers and directors. At the end of the day, no matter how comfortable the seat is, or how easy it is to park, or how fine the coffee is, if the quality of the play isn't good the stadium won't be full.

'As a forward I particularly like to see the creative, attacking players and goal-scorers. They are the ones who bring the crowds in but, having said that, it's not been easy for defenders, bearing in mind the new directives. In general I think the changes will be good for the game and encourage skilful players.

'I like to see players like Peter Beardsley and Chris Waddle, who are like good wine, and I love to see Alan Shearer, who reminds me of my old idol, Nat Lofthouse. I like to see youngsters coming through from the lower divisions; I like to see flank players, such as Ryan Giggs and Lee Sharpe and Jason Wilcox.

'We're lucky here to have United on our doorstep and Blackburn just up the road. I enjoy watching Cantona and I'm equally pleased to see the transformation of David Batty from midfield destroyer to midfield general. It's nice to see Kevin Keegan showing in management as he showed as a player. It's good to see his team playing so well up there.

'There's a lot in our game that is good but it's important that we don't paper over the cracks with not having to qualify for the next European Championship, think everything in our garden is lovely and miss out on another World Cup. The one good thing about increased foreign infiltration could be to emphasise the skill and technique which I believe is needed for international success.

'The direct style that our FA coaching department has been preaching will never, ever win you a World Cup. The day it does will be the death knell for football. Sometimes skill has been ignored for the benefit of strength and speed, all the way up. Our coaching system has been dominated by former schoolteachers and has not included enough former pros, to the extent that it's become discredited.

'England are now trying to get to youngsters aged nine and I'm worried that a coaching set-up that has only a two-week period for people to qualify and be able to coach at the very highest level is really an indication of how far we've fallen behind the rest of the world. Coaching has got to have a much more comprehensive approach, with ideas on diet, physiology, psychology and so on.'

So what else does Taylor's vision of the future for his union and football encompass? 'If we are not careful the FA is going to be led by the tail by the Premier League chairmen, who are solely concerned with what's right for their own clubs. Therefore, the FA needs to be much more professional. The Premier League must not be allowed to ignore what's happening in the Endsleigh League. That's why it's important you have the support of your top players when you have a crisis such as the Premier League breakaway. The Premier League players were 94/95 per cent behind the union, prepared to strike, prepared not to play in front of the cameras. This enabled our agreements to stay in place and our income from TV money to be increased and used for a better spread.

'I would hope that, as in golf, with the PGA, and tennis, with the Association of Tennis Professionals, the players themselves become much more like partners and are involved in the decision-making process. There should be a collective responsibility. There is a general feeling that players are just youngsters, that the bosses know best. Yet when it comes to tribunals I can tell you that the person who most impresses with his honesty and integrity isn't the chairman, or the director, or the manager, but the player who comes in on his own and says it as it is. And that's why I, for one, am pleased to be working for the players.'

CHAPTER 3

The Rule of Law

Neil Midgley, former FIFA referee, now FA match observer and League match assessor

A shrill blast of the whistle pulls up play on the far side to a reflex accompaniment of groans from the locals, but the former FIFA referee, sitting in the directors' box, nods approvingly and scribbles in his notebook. Neil Midgley, monitoring the performance of the match officials, points his pen towards the referee and whispers: 'He's a bit of a cocky character, a travel agent. He's a real Oldhamer. He's positive. Better than being a namby-pamby.'

The modern interpretation of the laws of the game, imposed in FIFA's edict and reiterated in England by an FA mandate, has been the source of fervent debate this past year. There is a feeling some referees, rather than players, have gone over the top. Above all, comes the cry: 'Let us have consistency.'

Over the course of a week the quest to raise refereeing standards has taken Midgley, as match observer, with the wider responsibilities that implies, to the Werder Bremen versus Maccabi Tel Aviv European Cup-Winners' Cup tie, to the Manchester United versus Everton Premiership clash and now, as a League assessor, to a corner of Cheshire where they will boast the oldest ground in the world as soon as tell you about their salt-mines. The venue: Drill Field. The match: Northwich Victoria versus Halifax Town in the Bob Lord Trophy, a knock-out competition for Vauxhall Conference clubs.

Midgley, from Bolton, has a comprehensive guide to what he should be looking for, under the headings: application of the laws, positioning, fitness, advantage, signals, stoppages, co-operation with linesmen, summary. He will write up a report on the officials and mark the referee, from one (totally unacceptable) to ten (faultless). In reality, the rating is likely to be from five (adequate) to eight (very good).

The 'Oldhamer' under scrutiny tonight is Gary Shaw, a referee considered promising and worthy of attention. 'He's side on and getting good positions,' Midgley says, 'but then it's easier when there's no aggro.'

One comment in Midgley's report will suggest Shaw might have instructed the Halifax goalkeeper to change his jersey, a rather fetching shade of violet, which Midgley feels clashes with the royal blue shirts of his colleagues. He also notes that a linesman is a little too hasty with his flag when a player drifting 'offside' is patently not 'active'.

Shaw becomes active, taking out his yellow card and booking a player for a foul – though certainly not violent – tackle from behind. 'Fair enough,' agrees Midgley. 'The idea is to encourage and protect skilful players. Defenders know they can't go clattering into forwards and the game is better, more appetising. In my opinion the FIFA directives have actually made refereeing easier – whether through fear or respect, I don't know. I go along with them if they are applied with commonsense. Players will co-operate if they see you have empathy. It's man management.'

Into the second half, Shaw is busier with his notebook and yellow card, Halifax's goal levelling the scores on aggregate and turning up the temperature. The visiting goalkeeper, well outside his area, impedes a forward but with cover at hand it is adjudged not to have been a goal-scoring opportunity. 'That's about right,' Midgley says. 'He could easily have been influenced by the home crowd. The mood can change when things go against the home team and so can the demands on the referee. Control and positioning are a bit of a science, but it can go to pot when you are chasing it.'

The teams are still level after 90 minutes and the voice on the public address system solemnly announces: 'There will now be 15 minutes each way of football.' The mandatory malcontent responds: 'You must be joking.'

The ladies responsible for catering in the cosy, wood-panelled boardroom have more pressing business. 'We've had to take the pizza out of the oven,' says one.

Few words go unheard when the attendance is 780, especially those directed at the referee. 'It's easier at the big games with the big crowds because then it's just a mass of noise,' Midgley says. 'I believe the referee's job overall gets easier the higher up you go. If you can come through this level you've a much better chance higher up because it's more skilful, players have more time on the ball.'

An exquisite piece of skill and stunning shot from Carwyn Williams win the tie for Northwich in extra time and at the end Midgley notes that the referee receives genuinely cordial handshakes from players of both teams. The contents of the report are confidential but Shaw will probably have a reasonable mark. 'We're not here to criticise but to assist,' Midgley stresses. 'Of course referees make mistakes, but fewer than players do and they have more good games than bad.'

Midgley, who retired from refereeing three years ago, speaks from bitter-sweet experience. 'I had good and bad, course I did. I had the 4–4 Everton-Liverpool Cup replay and the 1987 FA Cup final, when Coventry beat Spurs after extra time. Absolutely fabulous.

'I never gave a penalty that wasn't one, I don't care what anybody says about that, but I might have missed penalties. I certainly did in the Liverpool-Everton 0–0 game which led to the 4–4. Pat Nevin was brought down by Gary Ablett. I had a hopeless view of it and no idea, so I couldn't give it. When I saw the incident on television of course I could see it should have been a penalty. But I was honest about it. The irony is that we got the 4–4 out of it.

'I've had bad days when nothing would go right. I remember my first ever First Division game. I'd always aimed for this and when it finally came I couldn't believe I'd made it. The game was Aston Villa versus QPR. It wasn't easy to handle and no matter what I did I was unpopular with the crowd. After the match my wife, who was in the stand, told me that at one stage the entire row in front of her stood up and gave me the V-sign. I asked her what she did and she said she didn't want them to know who she was so she stood up and joined in.

'Ee, we've dined out on that one. There's always a silver lining. Life's too short to be too serious.'

Midgley, whose wit now earns him regular bookings on the after-dinner circuit, found his banter enabled him to develop a rapport with players. 'In that Cup final I'd decided on my tactics beforehand. I was going to let them know I was around in the first few minutes and, if they got the message, I'd back off and let them play. I was talking to them all the time but coming in only when I had to, and the lads were brilliant.

'It's psychology, really, handling players. If a couple of players started having a go at each other I'd say things like, "You've had one, and he's had one, that's one apiece. By the way, I normally have the winner." Or I would say, "Are you considering staying, because I'll be stopping till about quarter to five today?" Silly things, but it amused them and I won them over. It didn't mean I didn't caution or send people off when I had to. I did my share of that, as well. The players have to play it by the rules, just as the referees have to do what they are told.

'But if you treat people with a bit of respect, show you are human, eventually the word goes round that you're not a bad fellow. The way I did it stood me in good stead because I seemed to be quite successful at it. I find I'm welcome at grounds when I go around now and that's a nice feeling.

'I'm all for the quiet word, but up to a point. If it doesn't work, then you've got to take action. It's like telling somebody, "Take your hand out of the till but let me know when you've taken enough." You can't do that. There are those you can guide away from trouble, but there are those you can't. They just have to take the consequences.

'It was the same at school. It was always the same lads getting the cane. Similarly, it's always the same lads who seem to be in trouble on the field. I used to hear "This referee could cost me my job." To that I'd say "You've had 30 different referees this season, they can't all be wrong." When a player is suspended because he's accumulated a number of cautions, it's not the same referee who's been involved. So it's not a personality clash.

'Refereeing is a subject that will always have us hot under the collar, and that is its beauty as well as its beastly bit. I do believe that's part of the fun for people watching football. We'll never be seen to get it perfectly right. It's about opinions, just as no two people would pick the same England team.'

One question constantly gnaws away at logic here: Why DO they do it? What possesses an ostensibly normal human to subject himself or herself to the abuses that are now more familiar than an all-black referee's outfit? It cannot be the money. Perhaps it is a masochistic tendency; maybe the craving for power, fame, even infamy, an ego trip?

31

Midgley says: 'I started, as just about everybody else did, in the local league and it becomes a part of you. Eventually, if you are fortunate and have the ability, you get through to the top level. It's a great feeling, you know. You do it because you love football.

'It can't be an ego trip to go out at a Vauxhall Conference ground on a Tuesday night in the middle of winter, to be abused and booed and cat-called, then get in your car, drive all the way home, and then have to get up for work the following morning, where you're as likely to get more rubbish thrown at you as a pat on the back. That can't be an ego trip.

'But I will say that it's a great feeling when you run out at Old Trafford, or Wembley. I suppose it's just that we were not good enough to play for England. Once you get out there, you're on your own, you've got to do it, because you've still got those work mates to face the next day!'

Referees inevitably have to contend with the occasional petty jealousy at the day job, but although they require accommodating employers they use up their holiday entitlement to pursue their football ambitions. Midgley, sales manager with a battery firm he has worked at for 34 years, has also found his profile has taken him through business doors that might otherwise have been closed. 'I was so intent on doing well as a referee I would have been prepared to lose my job, anyway. I made myself time. When I got onto the international panel, the FIFA list, it became even more difficult. You could be away weeks at a time.

'I tell referees now to make themselves time. If it's good enough for the players, it's good enough for the referees. I tell them: "Don't go straight from work to a game but have the afternoon off, get your head down. I always did." Do you know why? Because the players did. "It's not always possible, but where you can arrange it, don't travel 150 miles on a Saturday morning, go the night before. The players do. Don't have steak pudding, chips, peas, bread and butter at one o'clock on a Saturday, because the players don't do that, you know? Then you won't go far wrong".'

That brings us, unerringly, to the subject of professional referees. Midgley says: 'Considering the time, effort and thought that goes into it, the approach is professional now. I didn't go on holiday with my wife for years. The problem is that you'd need a contract for five or ten years, because you couldn't afford to give up your job otherwise. But then the reward in any walk of life is for achievement, so it's no good saying, "You're on for ten years, pal, so you're all right." You can't do that, and it would block the system for those lads coming through.

'But I do believe there might eventually be a case for a panel of professional referees, probably the FIFA type, refereeing internationals and also coaching and instructing lower down the scale. I'm not sure who would want to give up his job for that, so you might not necessarily end up with the best referees, which defeats the purpose of the exercise.

'Professional or not, all you can do is get on with the job to the best of your ability. Then, when it's in the filing cabinet, leave it there. Just refer to it when you want to. I think we have some very good referees in this country, but I do feel some modern referees are too serious. They will say they enjoy it, but I'm not so sure they do. There's a lot of pressure now from within and without, and I'm not sure they can enjoy it the same as we did in the past.

'The problem now, I think, is that we have the Premier League referees in one camp, having their matches and their seminars and their message read out to them, and then we have the Football League with their meetings. At the Referees and Linesmen's Association we feel we should be doing the training for both Leagues, and then we can get uniform refereeing. As it is, we're not really being used. That's politics.'

Midgley believes the men with vast experience of controlling football at the highest level should have a stronger influence on refereeing guidelines and that a blanket system of assessment would help achieve greater consistency in the application and interpretation of the laws. All Premiership fixtures are covered by FA observers but not all Football League matches are attended by assessors.

'I have to put my hand on my heart and say the refereeing isn't consistent,' Midgley confides. 'I've heard so much against the assessing scheme but there will always be pressure on referees to be more consistent when we don't have independent assessments at every match. There are so many ex-referees who want to help, fellows who have been there and worn the T-shirt. Then I'm sure we'd get a more consistent and uniform application of the laws.

'I just hope that people in authority, who dictate the policies of football, will listen to what referees have to say because they do have a contribution to make. They shouldn't be making refereeing policy decisions when they are not referees themselves, and that's happening. I wouldn't like to think it's the cost. We've got nowt to gain.'

Even less than the referees, in fact. Midgley and the other 23 FA match observers are paid an insignificant fee, and expenses, for reporting on the general stewardship and organisation, as well as the officiating, at Premiership games, while observers at European ties receive expenses only, as do League match assessors. So why do THEY do it?

'I think we feel morally and duty bound to do it,' Midgley replies. 'We're trying to put something back into the game we love. Or else we're just crackers!'

Ah, we got there in the end. Our suspicions are confirmed.

CHAPTER 4

The Crying Game

Mike Walker, manager of Everton,
January to November 1994

They like to tell you of their football and wit on Merseyside: products of, and insulation against, a harsh environment. In more recent times the game and the folk in these parts have found it more difficult to raise a smile. Hillsborough, of course, would have torn the heart out of any community. The final death toll was 96. But since the year of that tragedy, 1989, when they went on to beat neighbours Everton in the FA Cup Final, Liverpool have been a team 'in transition'. Some would say that is a euphemism for 'in decline'. The secret of the club's unparallelled success was probably the fact that the side was constantly in transition. Every year they bought the best available players, ensuring the team never grew too old, stale or ineffective.

Into the 'Nineties, things were different. Kenny Dalglish, playing icon turned managerial icon, walked away from the pressures, and an FA Cup success could not spare his successor, Graeme Souness, another outstanding former player, the criticism which eventually forced him out.

Across Stanley Park, the house of Everton was even bleaker. The return of Howard Kendall as manager failed to turn back the clock to the mid-'Eighties. Bereft of talent and cash, the club lurched towards relegation. Howard, too, departed.

There was a feeling some of the humour had already gone; cynicism, envy, even naked hostility had become evident where once there was warmth and fun. Perhaps too many Liverpudlians too easily succumbed to setbacks, the spirit broken. The perception of a morose Merseyside, wallowing in grief, chip on shoulder, prompted one publication to dub it 'Self-pity City'.

The advent of 1994 offered Liverpool and Everton new managers and new hope. Roy Evans, a Liverpool devotee all his life, once a fan on the Kop, latterly a member of the backroom staff, always a relatively humble soul, followed the superstars in charge at Anfield and determined to retrieve some of the missing fundamentals, re-establish some of the old standards.

Over at Goodison Park, they summoned Mike Walker. He was not an Evertonian, as such, though there were suggestions he might have been as a lad. Anyway, he had made Norwich City a side admired and feared by the best in England and Europe, and if he could do that with such modest means surely he could revive Everton.

Optimism trickled again at Anfield. Come the 1994–95 season it flowed to the extent that it replenished Championship ambitions. At Goodison they were thankful to retain Premier League status after a tense final round of matches in the spring of '94, but autumn again loomed dark and forbidding. The historians dug deeper into the past to find a worse start to a season by the club until eventually they could not. Everton were nailed to the bottom of the table.

Only a few months after being a manager in demand, Walker was now one of the managers under pressure. He was not alone. The high stakes of the Premiership were straining the faith of boards across the nation. And this season, with four clubs to go down, nerves were particularly taut.

Sitting in his office at Everton's Bellefield training ground, this damp, unforgiving autumn day, Walker, a former goalkeeper, seems composed enough, covering the angles and parrying the shots. 'Of course it's not gone as well as I would have hoped,' he says. 'You never expect to be down at the bottom. But if you look at our games, it's not as if we've had a complete nightmare. But it takes time.'

Time, alas, is always at a premium for a football manager. The new regime at Everton – Peter Johnson took over as chairman in the summer – grows as restless as the natives. Many wonder if this 48-year-old Welshman peaked in the safe haven of East Anglia and now finds himself reaching too high. He contends otherwise and insists he has no regrets about taking on the challenge. He retains his faith in his ability and his chosen style of football, a style consistent, after all, with Everton's heritage.

Walker says: 'The start we've had has battered my pride but not my self-belief. I was at the top with Colchester and the same at Norwich, so this is new to me. But a little adversity makes you appreciate certain other things. There are two things you can do.

You can stand up and be counted and fight, or you can turn over and sink. There's no way I intend to sink.

'Everton have looked at the way Norwich played and thought, "He could be the fella." I think we were compatible. I don't see the need to change that way of playing. Forest got a lot of stick after one bad season. People were saying it was the football that cost them. That brand of football won them Championships and European Cups. It was selling Sheringham and Walker that cost them.

'All right, I played in the old Fourth Division and the Third and the Second, Under-23s for Wales. But I think you get better values when you come from the bottom. That doesn't bother me. I don't feel embarrassed now to be manager of a top club, rubbing shoulders with the Fergusons and Grahams. Many of the people who played at the top haven't got a clue. I'm now manager of Everton but it's not something that just happened. It took me 30 years to do it, through trial and error, mistakes, relegation and promotion. You learn as you go on.

'It's how you perceive the game. It doesn't mean because you were at the bottom you know nothing about the top. The principles that worked at Norwich were good enough to put us up there with the top teams, so why shouldn't they work here, where they've got better facilities in terms of finances to hit the top? I've always liked a passing game and I think I proved a point last year, in Europe, when Norwich beat Bayern Munich. Tactically, we worked it out and we did it. The teams who win the big prizes these days tend to play that way. Just look at the best teams in this country.

'I didn't have to come here. I could have stayed at Norwich and been comfortable for the next four or five years, but I didn't choose to do that. I knew there would be difficulties, but I wanted a crack at something where I thought we could win something, and that was my biggest bone of contention at Norwich. I didn't think they wanted to go on and win something.

'We're not kidding ourselves we're going to go out and tear up the League. We've got to lay the foundations and build something to last, not just waste money. It took Alex Ferguson seven years and £20 million to build that team at Man United. And it was only a good Cup run that saved him his job at one stage. Patience is important for a manager and those around him. Alex once told me to make sure I was single-minded and do what I think is right. You take advice from people you admire and respect.'

But if you grant the pedigree, can the demanding followers of this club be sure he shares their passion and commitment? Walker responds 'The expectations got through to me within five minutes of walking into the city. No danger. You only have to look at the last game of the season: 31,000 here on only three sides, 5,000 to 7,000 locked out, people crying when we were two down. Unbelievable.

'When I went shopping in the city for the first time it took me 40 minutes to go 200 yards. I stopped to talk and suddenly I was swamped. That's how passionate they are, but because of the passion they want it yesterday, and I can understand that. No, I wasn't an Everton fan, as has been said. I was born in Colwyn Bay but we moved when I was very young. But I used to go on about Alex Young and I remember the football Everton played at that time was excellent. So I do understand the feeling here and it does annoy me when people think you don't care about it. Believe me, nobody cares more than I do and my staff do.

'Any top manager will tell you it's a 24-hour-a-day, seven days-a-week job. Football is almost more important than family. It's marginal. You've got to have the enthusiasm as well as the ability. You can have some of the greatest players, but if they don't want to know, no chance. You're always a fan if you're really into it. If you're not, you might as well say goodbye, pack it in. I'm a fan.

'If I get it right, which is absolutely what I intend to do, there's no reason why we shouldn't at least emulate what we did in the 'Eighties, or what Howard did in the 'Eighties. That's the sort of thing you've got to go back to, because the club is big enough and the fans are enthusiastic enough. It's all there.

'There should be two big clubs here, bouncing off each other again, and I don't mean to be disrespectful to Tranmere, because they've done brilliantly. But we need that competition. It's definitely a hot bed here, but for the last five or six years it's been going downhill. You can't change it overnight. You need to stop it going downhill, start building, and start going up again.

'To be fair, the difference now at Everton, compared with recent years, is that we are able to purchase the best, and if you are purchasing the best you appreciate that it is very difficult to shift the best. If I went to try to buy a Shearer or a Cole I wouldn't get much encouragement. But it's no good to just go and sign three or four players and find six months later that they are not right, so we've taken our time. Despite what people say, we've actually been quite selective.'

Walker recruited the winger, Anders Limpar, the midfield player, Vinny Samways, the defender, David Burrows, and the Nigerian World Cup striker, Daniel Amokachi. The Brazilian, Muller, was to have been next, but that deal fell through when the player demanded his tax be paid by Everton.

The signing of Limpar was the first to raise eyebrows. Walker says: 'I would like to see him hold the width a bit more, because that's what we got him for. As he proved against Villa and Forest, when he does keep the width, one on one, he's a force, definitely a danger. He can win games and sometimes he can frustrate you, but we needed that little extra buzz at the time.'

Samways? 'We're well pleased with Samways. We needed a passer in the team, to bring some variation, and as we get better players, or we increase the squad, then obviously it's going to be an asset for us. We've done a lot of work on trying to get the passing right, because although they thought they were a passing team, they weren't that good, and there have been distinct signs of improvement on that side.'

Burrows arrived as part of an exchange deal that returned Tony Cottee to West Ham United. 'It was a convenient way. They didn't have the money to pay for Tony. It's not often things fall so sweetly into place and I'm delighted to get David. Not only is he a very good player but he's also enthusiastic and he competes. I needed a bit of that.'

And then came Amokachi, at £3 million the most expensive as well as adventurous piece of business conducted by Walker. 'I've no worries about him. He's packed in a hell of a lot of experience already, he's been playing in European competition, he's won the League with Bruges and he's been in the World Cup. He's not the sort of player who's going to be fazed. He's strong and got good pace. He also speaks better English than some of our Scouser lads!'

Walker was always conscious of deficiences in attack, but a sudden leakage of goals caused unanticipated alarm. 'All the clever dicks are getting on saying, "What about the defence?" Yeah, I'm aware of that. It's causing me anxiety and we've been working very hard on the back four, along with the midfield players doing the right thing, and the front men. If we can't tighten up we'll have to look at that.'

The potential of defender David Unsworth, underlined by his graduation to the England Under-21 team, encourages Walker to believe: 'He's saved the club, probably, £3 million. The thing that really convinced me was that last game last season, against Wimbledon, rough and ready, a real crunch game, big crowd, and the kid never turned a hair.

'We've got one or two more youngsters coming through now. Our reserves looked certainties for relegation last year and this year they've started unbeaten. Unfortunately the most important team hasn't won, but it's just a matter of time.'

There are those who suggest goalkeeper Neville Southall's time is up and that Walker should try to prise his son, Ian, from Tottenham. Walker senior says: 'Ever since I came to the club I've been advised Neville was over the top, ready to go and so on. I will decide that and I'm sure Neville will realise when he's had it. I still feel he's saving more games than he's costing us. If that proves a problem then, as with anybody else, we'll have to look at it. My boy, yes, I think he's blossomed into a half decent 'keeper, but I think it's a bit premature to start talking about whether he'd come here. At the moment we've got other things to sort out.

'We've had to change some attitudes, as well. As I've said, for a few years now it's been going down here, and that's as hard as anything. It's getting heads right to do it. Certainly most of the players are quite capable of competing with the best. The fans here deserve success again. They've waited a long time and maybe a few weeks like this won't matter as long as we get it right. But that's the most important thing, getting it right.

'I think it's important in this city for both clubs to be up there. Suddenly Roy Evans has got thrown into the hot seat over there and I've come from out of the city, and hopefully we can stay together in League terms. Most people here want to see Merseyside football back on top, competing with the best, and I'll drink to that.'

It was last orders for Walker at Everton. He was shown the door in November, the month when Premiership managers were reeling like drunks. Osvaldo Ardiles was sacked by Tottenham Hotspur and Ron Atkinson by

Aston Villa. Gerry Francis left Queens Park Rangers and joined Tottenham, while Brian Little took over at Villa after quitting Leicester.

Walker described the timing of his dismissal as 'bizarre'. After 17 defeats in the first 32 matches under his stewardship, the team were unbeaten in three and had registered their first victory of the season only a week earlier. The arrival of Duncan Ferguson from Rangers was too late to influence the fate of Mike Walker.

He was succeeded by Joe Royle, returning to his spiritual home from Oldham Athletic, and Everton had something to drink to immediately. They beat Liverpool. They also went on to avoid relegation and won the FA Cup, defeating the holders, Manchester United, 1–0 in the final.

Liverpool won the Coca Cola Cup and beat Everton in the negotiations for the record £8.5 million signing of Stan Collymore.

CHAPTER 5

The Deadpan Striker

Graham Kelly, chief executive of the Football Association

Graham Kelly is moving from desk to desk, hand held out, taking money from his staff, his face a bowl of contentment. Is there no limit to the greed of the FA? No end to the commercial connivance of the bosses at Lancaster Gate? In fact, Kelly is collecting his earnings from a 20-mile sponsored walk, the proceeds to aid cancer research. He had completed his charity work the previous Saturday in time to get to a match in the afternoon. Late that night he was on duty for the televised Cup draw, so not surprisingly he fluffed a couple of his lines.

A lot of things about Kelly are surprising. Somehow, this charity walk is. It shouldn't be, of course it shouldn't. But we have this image of Mr Glum, who sits at that table, dolefully introducing the draw, and who occasionally emerges from his bunker, stands on the pavement and takes more flak over another embarrassing episode in the calamitous saga of our game's governors.

Apart from refuting many of the charges levelled at his organisation, he reveals an unlikely sense of fun and adventure behind that grey public mask. Here, would you believe, is an exponent of the one-liner, a master of the last third one-two.

You would certainly need some release if you were in Kelly's position. That pavement in Lancaster Gate has been awash in scandals and allegations fed from tributaries throughout English football. There have been stories of bribes, bungs and drugs. There has been the controversy over Terry Venables' appointment as England coach and disciplinary measures against his former club, Tottenham, over illegal payments. All this and the usual quota of power struggles and accusations of incompetence.

Back in his own office – modest, MFI-ish, compared with Gordon Taylor's – Kelly is in familiar mode, fending off the onslaught. For a start, the man who first put himself in the firing line when he succeeded Alan Hardaker as Secretary of the Football League, in 1979, does not like his little workplace being referred to as a bunker, or the suggestion that the FA is accident-prone.

'I don't think it is a bunker, but it occasionally gets represented that way,' he says. 'Things are a lot more difficult these days. There are a lot more difficult issues, people contest things more readily than they used to, so it can be more complex, more complicated. Lawyers are involved, big money. Money has exploded. We've been very active. We've instituted the Premier League and things are more dynamic in every respect. We have a turnover of nearly £50 million a year, whereas it was about £6 million before I came here, in '88/'89. There's been a real boom with commercial interests and just the general range of activities we've got involved in. We get involved in so much more – women's football, centres of excellence, we've changed the scheme whereby clubs can have much more access to young players now. There's much more going on.

'The commercialism is not at the expense of the poorer teams because the Football League are much better off now than they were previously. The clubs outside the Premier Division get a much bigger share of a bigger cake in so far as television is concerned. Had we not split the Premier, they would not necessarily have had the same cake. One cannot ignore the commercial realities of life and if we wish to become involved in developing facilities and grounds and so on and so forth, we have to generate the revenue in order to plough it back into the development of the game. That's what the FA is all about, trying to make improvements at every level.

'I am very happy with the way the FA has made progress in the interests of all its clubs. I don't think there's any problem with sponsorship. "The FA Cup, sponsored by Littlewoods Pools" – I don't see that as selling the birthright. It seems quite straightforward, it's not changing the name, it's not selling our souls or destroying our heritage or whatever you may care to say.

'It is much broader than we see on the back pages of the papers. The high profile cases – Paul Merson, Bruce Grobbelaar, Spurs – are only the tip of the iceberg.'

As we speak, newspaper allegations of match-fixing against Grobbelaar are being investigated. Merson, the Arsenal player, escaped punishment but agreed to go to a rehabilitation centre for six weeks after confessing to the use of cocaine, a class 'A' drug. The FA were widely accused of being too lenient with him. Kelly says: 'I answer that quite simply by pointing to the tough regime that he has to go through. He's not got an easy ride to rehabilitate himself. If the wheels come off he gets dealt with very severely by the FA. He gets charged with misconduct if he doesn't see the course through. In any event he's going to be out of the game for a period so suspension is irrelevant. And he has to contribute financially. He pays a significant proportion of the rehabilitation himself. So I reject wholeheartedly the concept that he's got off lightly.

'In any event the people who argue for retribution and punitive action don't recognise that that's no longer regarded as the best way of dealing with these situations. The expert advice is rehabilitation care. One of the undertakings he has given us is that if we required it, he would undertake educational work when rehabilitated to help kids realise the dangers of drugs. He said everybody knew the dangers of smoking, but with cocaine it wasn't widely known what the medical problems might be. He'd be happy to learn about that and pass it on to children.'

Before the start of the 1994–95 season, Spurs were fined £1,500,000, had 12 League points deducted and were banned from the FA Cup for making illegal payments. The points penalty was later reduced to six and, after taking their case to arbitration, Spurs had all their points, and their place in the FA Cup, restored. The fine was confirmed.

Lancaster Gate's displeasure is evident, but Kelly finds consolation in the tribunal's affirmation of the FA's authority. 'What has been made clear is that the FA have the absolute power to deduct points and ban clubs from Cup competitions,' Kelly says. 'If the events of the past six months have proved anything, it is that such punishments are the ones clubs care about most passionately. They are the real deterrents and the FA's resolve to fight financial abuses, wherever they are, and in whatever form they take, is now stronger than ever.'

And so to the bungs, back-handers said to have been received in the transfer of a number of foreign players to English clubs. These claims are also under investigation, though Kelly says: 'The problem points at the dangers of having uncontrolled agents floating around the game with their activities not subject to any scrutiny. That is now changing. FIFA have brought in new rules which are applicable from 1 January 1995, whereby agents have to be licensed. They have to come to the national association for interview and put down a bond. So, hopefully, their activities will be more closely controlled. Without that licence, an agent can't operate. Put it this way, those in football who deal with an unlicensed agent will be breaking football rules.'

And so to Venables, put in charge of the national team despite allegations of financial irregularities, as featured on *Panorama* television programmes. Kelly admits: 'I have to say that Terry was somewhat of a gamble given that we appointed him while all sorts of allegations were flying around. We preferred to accept his word. Nothing I've heard or seen since then has persuaded me to doubt his word in any way and we concentrated solely on his ability as a football coach, in which area he has an almost unrivalled reputation. So we hope he will be able to concentrate more on football and less on my learned friends. I personally felt that *Panorama* weakened, rather than strengthened, their case vis-a-vis Terry Venables, by scraping the barrel with some of the characters they featured in the second programme. That's a personal opinion.'

But how do you take it when the FA are slagged off time and again? 'It all depends what it is. I always say that if there is an issue to be faced, let's face it, let's look the criticism in the eye and discuss the issues honestly and openly – if it's agents in football, or it's alleged bribery, or if it's drug-taking or whatever it is. Yes, it dismays me that football is being denigrated in this way, but there's no alternative but to tackle the issues head-on and get them out of the way so that they don't recur in the future.'

What about the future of England? 'I think we've got a good coach who knows what he wants from the players, he knows the strengths and weaknesses of English football better than most and he's more capable than most of getting the most successful team. I'm very happy with this new kind of structure on the coaching side – integration, getting everybody behind the one unit, the technical control board or the technical director. I think it is something that was long needed. The PFA are thinking on similar lines and there's almost a danger unanimity will break out in football! At the moment the situation with the technical director is an open book. It could be anybody provided that anybody has a proven record and is charismatic and capable of doing the job. He doesn't have to be English.'

There has never been unanimity over the concept of the Premier League. Three years on, Kelly believes it has been confirmed as 'a great idea'. He expands: 'When you look around at the grounds and the stadia, the entertainment being provided in the Premier League, I don't think it would have happened with the old First Division. It's about clubs having the ability to react to the Taylor Report. I think we've created an environment where top clubs can compete with the best on the Continent both on the field and off the field. What you had before was a structure which embodied the big club and the small clubs and neither were happy with it.'

Surely, though, our clubs have not competed on the Continental field as well as hoped? 'I think you have to analyse each case. I think, by and large, we are capable of competing with the best in Europe. Our best have done reasonably well considering we had five years out of Europe. I think a lot of the players in those teams are players who would have benefited enormously from two or three years in Europe at the time we were banished. I think that's a big factor people sometimes overlook.

'I think we've also been affected by the foreigners rule. I'm a great believer in restrictions on foreign players because I think only that way can you guarantee the young players will come through, by making sure they are not blocked by a surfeit of foreign players. I appreciate you learn to play alongside Klinsmann or Cantona but if there are too many foreign players the talent won't come through. I agree with Gordon on that one.

'I certainly believe there's too much football at the top level and I think it was a retrograde step for the Football League to go back up from 20 clubs to 22. It's like drawing teeth to try and get them to reduce the number. We're coming down to 20 after three years and the pressure is then on for a further reduction to 18. The anomaly is in this UEFA situation where they are encouraging a maximum of 18 clubs in a top division yet at the same time promoting the Intertoto Cup in the summer. It's a strange one.'

Turning to Wembley – or better still, away from Wembley, if they can't provide adequate toilets. 'Ideally I'd like to see England having the chance of going to the provinces more,' Kelly says, 'but that's a very complex subject because there's a lot of revenue needed, a lot of capital expenditure required for Wembley, or alternatively for a new stadium. Manchester are very committed and I think they will have a new stadium. Birmingham are interested. Certainly Wembley has a major attraction. Foreigners like to play at Wembley. It has the mystique. And toilet facilities are getting a bit better.'

Now come on Graham, what really lurks behind this calm, serious exterior? Do you ever let yourself go? 'Only when I'm playing football,' he replies, never altering the tone of his voice or the expression on his face. Suddenly, though, the mask slips a little. A flicker of a grin. The 49-year-old journeyman striker with a little excess baggage concedes: 'I've got to this stage in my career where I'll play for anyone who'll have me. Last season I played for four different teams without really finding my level. I played for Chris Turner's team on Sunday mornings. He's chief executive of Peterborough now and I live in the area. They go round the villages on Sunday mornings and I often get a game for them. I play up front – free rein. I hold it, just knock it five yards and then look for a touch in around the six-yard area. Mark Hughes is probably a good analogy, albeit I'm a trifle more creative. [*Another, more expansive grin.*] I played with Junior in San Francisco. Brilliant, absolutely brilliant. I don't know what he says about me. And I play a small-sided game once a week out in Hyde Park here, just a kickabout with some lads from the National History Museum. So that's when I let my hair down.

'But then I enjoy my job. Every minute of it. One of the nicest parts is getting around and meeting people. I get to some very strange grounds nowadays. I'll argue with fans behind the goal at some nondescript game. In the old days it used to be the four divisions, sit next to the chairman and that was it. But now I can wander around and get to some of the little grounds. Occasionally I get stick. At the start I probably did get one or two who had a go. I usually try and convert them by half-time. I just argue the point, either say they don't know what they're talking about or agree with them. That often takes them off-guard.

'You have to sit down at the top games, of course, and you've got to give the fans more comfort there. I love to go to the top grounds, with a capacity crowd and see a good game, and I do so regularly. It's a different experience. I know it's helter-skelter sometimes but I think, given the speed, that the skills of the players are tremendous.

'I was born in Blackpool and still look for the Blackpool results, but I wouldn't say I was a fan. When I was at the League I certainly couldn't describe myself as a Blackpool fan because it was so close to our offices at Lytham. Now, at the FA, where we have 40-odd thousand clubs, I don't think it matters that much if I say I look for Blackpool's result on a Saturday night. It's probably less likely to upset people than if I said United or Spurs. Anyway, they wouldn't expect me to say I was a Spurs fan, not at the moment!

'I have very little time for anything outside the game. I read anything I can pick up in an airport – magazines, crime stories, courtroom dramas. I like variety theatre. I've seen Alan Price, Ken Dodd and it's Jimmy Tarbuck tonight. Nothing avant-garde. Anything to do with comedy, anything humorous I enjoy. I like that element of after-dinner speaking. You inevitably have to do a bit of that as part of the job. I don't say I'm in great demand the length and breadth of the country, but I have my moments – deadpan delivery, the old one-liners.

'This was one of my more notable performances,' he says, reaching for the trophy on his desk. It is inscribed: '*When Saturday Comes* 1992/93 Readers Awards. The person who has done the most damage to football in the recent past – Graham Kelly.'

He goes on: 'I don't know why they gave me that. I suspect they didn't have a poll, they had a quick chat over a pint in the pub one night and decided I was up for an award, along with Harry Harris, Jimmy Hill, Alan Sugar and some others. My people here in the office said that if I went along to collect the award they'd take the proverbial, but they'd do it if I didn't, so I said I'd go. I didn't mind.

'I was the only one who turned up in person to collect the award. It was at a comedy club in Camden Town, a dingy place and there were about 300 of them in there. It was an interesting night, alternative comedy. I turned up in dinner jacket and black tie, like a proper awards evening. I went on stage and they all started heckling and booing. Then I pulled out my acceptance speech from my pocket, about a dozen sheets of paper, and started out, "This has really taken me by surprise, I didn't expect this award," and there were tears running down my cheeks. That magazine will hardly criticise me now.'

Surely he must accept he is there to be mocked, shot at and disliked? 'I think I'm knocking at the door of that category, yes. I think the higher profile the FA has taken, or had thrust upon it, since I've been here has probably put me up there – or down there, whichever way you look at it.'

He must be in danger of becoming a cult figure. 'Somebody said that to me when I went to get that award. He said they liked me really. They just might take the proverbial now and then . . .'

CHAPTER 6

Nice Little Earner

Eric Hall, agent

Barely a Route One ball from the FA's headquarters is the home and office of Eric Hall, football agent and as such apparently the Nemesis of the authority. We are just off the Edgware Road, in, would you believe, Star Street. We find the Georgian-look again but, unlike Gordon Taylor's neighbourhood, there's a faded authenticity here.

Hall works from a tiny basement room, his simple desk facing a television permanently tuned in to Teletext. Remote control in one hand, telephone in the other, cigar in mouth: the image he is happy to portray. So, too, that of the fast-talking Mr Fixit: London Jew, loud clothes, urgent mannerisms. A small man, he delights in being called 'monster' and adding 'ish' to a word for special effect. All part of the image, all part of the sell.

He has also been portrayed as a parasite and a cancer. Usually referred to as football's 'most controversial agent', he has been accused by an England striker of giving agents a bad name. Some of his clients, agitating for transfers, are said to have been afflicted by 'the Eric Hall hamstring'. He is quite partial to 'Mr Pickford – the removal agent'.

Whatever his image or his label, he has more than 30 players, including Dennis Wise, of Chelsea, Tim Sherwood, of Blackburn, Dean Holdsworth, of Wimbledon, and Jamie Redknapp, Neil Ruddock and John Scales, all of Liverpool, on his books. And he is busy. 'I'm a one-man orchestra,' he says. 'My role in the game – it's an old cliché of mine now – is to make the poor players rich and the rich players richer. And give them the right advice, of course.'

Hall is relatively new to handling footballers, but then he is relatively new to football. 'I've been in this business only about seven years. Showbiz I've been in since I was 11 years old and I'm over 50 now. I've been around showbiz people all that time. I was a child actor, a bad child actor, monster bad, and at 15 I went into the music business. I was packing parcels, me and Reg Dwight, who became Elton John. We started together in the business and off it went from there.

'I switched to football by accident, in a strange way, really. It involved Terry Venables. I've known Terry since I was 16. He was a young kid at Chelsea. One of my bosses was very friendly with the Chelsea players and after training they used to come down to his offices in Tin Pan Alley, Denmark Street, which in those days was a bubbly street. Everybody was down there – Cliff Richard, loads of 'em.

'I was involved with Mark Bolan, of T-Rex, the last couple of years of his life. [*Name-droppers, try to beat that little lot in a few lines.*] I'd known him many years before that but I was actually working with him at the end of his life. After he was killed in a car crash I had to go to Granada TV studios in Manchester for a tribute show. I came back to London that night, still very depressed and down, and went to a club in Berkley Square, and met Terry, and he shot me off to a place in Epping, a country club, for some function. I didn't want to go but Terry persuaded me to.

'Anyway, I met this guy at the bar there, called Steve. I told him what I did, and he said how about being an agent in football? I said, "Are you mad? I don't understand football." He said, "You don't have to to do what I'm talking about." Turned out I was talking to Steve Perryman. He was then captain of Tottenham. I don't believe in luck, you create your own luck, but Steve Perryman had known me two minutes and wants to know if I'll be his agent.

'I really wasn't that interested, so I gave him a tester. I gave him my number but didn't take his. If you want somebody you get him, don't you? So I thought if he's really keen – after all, we'd had a few beers – he'll call. He did call me and we met in the West End. There seemed to be more pluses than minuses and I became his agent. And that was it. All of a sudden I was a football agent.

'I've now got 30 to 40 players, a lot of big names from the Premier League but also people in the lower divisions. You get them because you never stop grafting. More come to me now than they did three, four, five years ago, yes, of course. I'm not being flash. I get phone calls. A player rings, "Can you get me a club?" But I still chase players. If I fancy someone, I will go out and chase them. I won't say I am the best agent – I AM the best agent, but I ain't going to say that ...'

But you just did.

'I know, it's the old showbiz trick – don't say it but still say it,' Hall returns, a triumphal grin spreading across his face. 'But I am the most famous agent, that's a fact.'

And the most controversial?

'Well, I don't think I am. People say I'm controversial. They say I'm flamboyant and controversial, but I can't see that. I wear bright jackets and I wear, normally, bright ties. This one's not too bright.'

How about a parasite, even a cancer?

'Tell you a story about that. I did the players' pool for Wimbledon when they played Liverpool in the FA Cup final, 1988, and Sam the Man [*Sam Hammam, Wimbledon's owner*] – to be fair, I love him, we're monster mates – he never really knew about agents then. This club from non-League, suddenly a First Division club – before the Premier, of course, this – and they were new to all this, now in the Cup final. At Wembley! Anyway, I represented John Fashanu and he asked me to look after the players' pool, on behalf of all the lads, you know, doing the business. Great for me, to look after the whole lot. It's a shame, really, for some poor agent who works all year on a player, suddenly it comes to the big Cup final day and he's blown out, that Eric Hall steps in.

'So, Sam says he doesn't want me doing the players' pool. He said he'd do it. I said, "Sam, you can't do it, you're the chairman, the owner, you can't work on behalf of the players." He says, "Baby, baby, I will do it, there won't be a conflict." I then explain to him he really can't do it, that there are other things he's got to do for himself and for the club.

'He was actually very frightened about it and he said in the papers he didn't want this Eric Hall, that he knew my reputation and didn't want me getting hold of the players, I was like a cancer and he didn't want it spreading through his club. But then three or four weeks later he apologised. He realised he shouldn't have said that. He realised I did a hell of a lot of hard work for the players.

By the time the Cup final was over, as well as Fash I had Andy Thorn, Dave Beasant and Dennis Wise.'

Bobby Gould, the then Wimbledon manager, was dismayed by Hall's influence on Wise, who resorted to a campaign of mischievous pranks, including setting off fireworks from the team's hotel, in his attempts to be released by the club. That incident was referred to in a television programme about agents and featuring, in particular, one Eric Hall. Gould reached the conclusion that Hall should have stayed in music.

Hall replies: 'To be fair, it was the first time I heard that story. I phoned Dennis after the show and asked him what this fireworks business was about. He said, "I never told you, Monster" – he calls me monster – he said, "I just had a bit of fun at the hotel." But I swear to you, I never knew about that. I knew he was up to one or two little tricks, trying to get sent home and get Gould to say, "You can go, we don't want you at this club." But it never worked initially. It worked eventually because he got away to Chelsea.'

In the programme, another agent posed the question: Is Hall good for the game? Hall says: 'I think I am good for footballers and, yeah, I believe I am good for the game. It's relative. But I am certainly good for footballers, yeah. I can't really believe in the old saying, "Any publicity is good publicity", but my concern is not what the public, or journalists or even chairmen, up to a point, think about Eric Hall. It's the players. Eric Hall is good at his job, for the players.'

And how much do they pay for his services? 'I take 20 per cent commercially, and on transfers, or contract negotiations, put it that way, forget the word transfer, I will say, "If you get this, I want that." It's never near 20 per cent. That's a fact, hand on heart. Everybody thinks I'm monster rich. I make a living, I can afford to smoke cigars, big monster ones, and I can afford to go out and have a big night. I certainly can't see myself retiring on the money I'm earning for at least another 30 years.'

Agents, as we have heard, must now be licensed, yet as we speak, less than a month from the date the new regulations are to take effect, Hall insists he has had no official notification of the requirement. 'Nobody's told me and nobody's told other agents I've spoken to. Obviously we have to be informed personally. How do I know I've got to go to the FA if they don't tell me? I get a letter once a year telling me my TV licence has got to be renewed and I send in my money. I'm quite a high profile agent. They do know I exist. There's probably hundreds of agents around, what I hear, but six or seven whose names they should know. I ain't being flash, but I'm definitely one of them.

'I've not been covered by any rules, I've not been under the jurisdiction of anybody. I've made my money but I pay taxes, I pay my VAT. If a club wants to work with me and they're not supposed to, they are breaking the rules, not me.

'Clubs come to me. They say they want to move a player but won't put him on the transfer list, so they come to me. If I want to get a player a new club I'll use the papers, I admit that. It's like selling records. If you want a new release plugged you go to the radio stations, don't you? I'm honest. Ask me a question, and I answer. I don't mind saying I will use the media to let everyone know if my player is available.'

Another accusation levelled at Hall is that he does not necessarily get his players the right moves to enhance their football careers, that he is more interested in the fast buck. 'That's a load of rubbish,' he says, unequivocally. 'Give you a for instance. I have this kid, Nick Forster. He played for Gillingham, scored buckets of goals, sensational kid. He could have gone to Blackburn, he could have gone to West Ham. In my little knowledge of the game I felt, because I took advice from pros I know, that the best move for him, at that age, was not to go to a Premier club, where he might be in the reserves for a couple of years, but to Brentford. He went there and obviously got less money. So I can't be accused of that.

'Here's how it is with players moving, hand on heart. If a player's got a problem, I will say to him, "Go and discuss it with your manager, or your chairman." If there is no solution I would say it is in the best interests of everybody that the player leaves the club. If you're at Safeways, supposed to be serving on the bacon counter but instead you're sitting around twiddling your thumbs, you're better off going and getting a job at Woolworths.

'I look after my players. Going back to that Cup final and Sam the Man. It was unbelievable. Wimbledon winning the Cup, beating Liverpool! Dennis Wise was probably getting about £300, a week then. I could understand. They got crowds of 3,000 or 4,000 for a League match. But the players had become stars overnight and at the Press conference on the Saturday night, Sam says, "I know, baby, my players are not on big wages, like the big clubs, but any of them can come and knock on my door and if they are not happy with their deal, I'll let 'em leave." My players asked me what they should do, so I got them to knock on his door. He did it himself.'

Hall makes no pretence at being a football aficionado. 'I enjoy football, I don't understand it,' he says. 'I know when somebody gets a penalty and when a goal's scored. But I'm terribly short-sighted. I'm vain, too, so I don't wear glasses. So far this season I've been to three matches – Brentford-Birmingham to see young Nicky, then QPR-Liverpool, and last Saturday Sam the Man invited me to Wimbledon-Blackburn. I said to somebody, "Who scored that?" He said, "Are you sure, it was Mark Atkins. You're his agent." I can't see, I can't see. Terry's wife bought me these opera glasses for my birthday!'

'With players, if I don't like 'em I don't have 'em. I believe I'm the best and I don't have a contract with anybody. I don't need contracts ...'

We are interrupted by a telephone call. Tim Sherwood is on the line, distraught because his girlfriend has called off their engagement after a magazine article alleged he had close encounters with Britt Ekland at Hall's birthday party. Hall assures the Blackburn captain he is on the case, demanding an apology. 'That's what we want, not money,' he stresses.

One distinguished client consoled, we turn to another: Dennis Wise. 'He's a star. We're very close, as I am with all my clients. He's got older and wiser, which happens. I've got to give credit to Glenn Hoddle [*the Chelsea manager*]. He gave Dennis the captaincy. Dennis loved it. He said, "I'm captain, monster. Can't believe it. Made me captain." He's been a Chelsea supporter all his life. So I think that helped him. His ability to play had been great. I said before, I'll never interfere on the football side. I'd never say to a player, "You should play on the left side, not the right" or, "You should be playing up front, not centre-half."

'Off the field is different. Like that video with Vinny Jones. I've been involved with people, ideas for me to do things for Dennis, and I've turned them down. I don't even let Dennis know about them. If somebody phones me and says, "You handle Vinny, I've got this hard man video about how you can break people's legs without the referee seeing", I'd say, "You are mad. On your bike." It wouldn't have gone any further.

'With Dennis, like this week, Christmas time, it's the old showbiz thing: If you're not working Christmas time, you should go become a bus driver. If you can't make a few bob at Christmas, when can you? Like today, we're doing a picture thing, Dennis the Menace, for the *Sunday People*, dress him up and everything. It might sound a silly thing to do but that's his image. He's doing a thing for *Today* newspaper, with his nieces and nephews, something for the *Sun* newspaper, and *Question of Sport* on Sunday.

'It's taken him ten years to become a star overnight. His football has got him there, but he's got a tremendous little cheeky face and, being from the showbiz world, I look for something as well as the football side. I check them out. They may have a great image, a great whatever, and be a schmuck and never get in the side, so you don't really want them. But I do look for that image situation. When I first got Dennis I knew then he was a star. I didn't know if he could play football or not but people I spoke to said he could. He's made it: Chelsea captain, playing for England ...'

Just one thing, Eric, he's lost the Chelsea captaincy. (Over an incident with a taxi driver which resulted in a court case.)

'He'll probably have it back by the time this book comes out!'

CHAPTER 7

Living the Dream

Bryan Robson, player-manager of Middlesbrough

Many areas claim to be football hotbeds, but few with greater conviction, or justification, than the North-East of England. The fervour in these parts is as legendary as some of the players reared here. Much of that talent, however, has found fulfilment elsewhere. The Charlton brothers, Bobby and Jack, moved away as boys to be acclaimed by other tribes and other regions. More recently, Alan Shearer launched his career on the South Coast. Some who played for Newcastle United were lured to distant clubs, even distant lands: Paul Gascoigne and Chris Waddle, for example.

But then the recent past has held out too little promise for gifted, ambitious young men in the North-East. The exodus of the better players reflected the economic plight as well as football under-achievement. The closure of pits and shipyards savaged entire communities. The spirit, though, remained defiant, sustaining the people as it sustained their forebears in times of even deeper crisis. It has always been evident among football supporters of Newcastle and Sunderland. And even hardened, experienced pros will tell you they have trembled in big Cup matches at Middlesbrough.

Now the passions are driven not merely by blind faith but by the genuine prospect of success and more success. Optimism is rampant, sweeping all the way down from Tyneside – though as yet bypassing Wearside – to the 'Southern' border of the North-East, Teesside. Sir John Hall and Kevin Keegan have transformed St James' Park from a den of frustration to a palace of plenty. Visions of glory are in focus again, not simply fantasies to tantalise the soul. Images of renaissance are vivid at Middlesbrough, too: a thrusting, refurbished team and a new stadium fit for heroes. Right across this scarred landscape, they are again living the dream.

The forces projecting Boro are Steve Gibson, a young business dynamo, and Bryan Robson, like Keegan a former England captain and a player capable of galvanising the qualities around him with unbridled commitment. In truth, Robson was even more of a leader on the pitch than Keegan was. Through the 'Eighties he was acknowledged as the nearest to the complete midfield player we were likely to get. He had everything and gave everything. He was Manchester United's and England's Captain Marvel.

So, in his first season of management – player-management, to be precise – what else would you expect but to see his team leading the contest for promotion to the Premier League? The script also has it Robson will develop into the natural successor to Alex Ferguson at United, or perhaps to Terry Venables, with England, and Boro will have to lump it.

Robson does not necessarily see it that way. Injuries and setbacks, as well as victory and honour, have been fellow travellers through his momentous playing career, and the extremes of experience and emotion have insulated him against megalomania. The famed fighter, the irrepressible, inspirational skipper is also a pragmatist. Robson always was his own man and chooses to concentrate his attention on fundamental matters, distancing himself from fanciful objectives and conjecture. And if he can live the dream of the North-East, who's to say he won't prefer to stay? Not Robson.

'Yes, the expectations are high,' Robson says, looking a trifle strange if not ill at ease, rocking in his chair, behind his desk at Ayresome Park. 'But to me it's nothing different to what I was used to for 13 years at United. Every season you start there, the expectation is to win the League, so you learn to come to terms with the downfalls. So many things in this game are taken out of your hands – injuries, suspensions, all at the wrong time. You see a player you want to sign and find he's not available, so you try to get somebody who's similar but that is like hitting your head against a brick wall.'

Welcome to management!

Robson, of course, was always going to be welcome to the management profession. He might have gone to Wolverhampton Wanderers, he could have gone to many a club, even purely as a player. Eventually he agreed to take on Boro, and his early progress has reinforced that judgment.

He says: 'The club finished tenth in the First Division last season, so I think we've started better than I could have dared hope for. The chairman gave me a bit of money, I brought in a few players and so far we've been getting the improvement I'm looking for. As long as you know you've done your best, and you've seen an improvement within the club, I feel that's all I can do.

'Of course I'm conscious of the comparison with Keegan because everybody mentions it all the time. He's done a great job at Newcastle, but that's Newcastle. I just blinker myself here and if I can improve this club on half the scale Keegan's done at Newcastle, then I'll be delighted. I don't think I'll have the resources Keegan's had at Newcastle but the chairman at this club is determined that if we achieve promotion we'll not settle for just staying there.

'Other managers have told me it's very important to have a chairman who supports you but stays out of the way and lets you get on with it. So far I've been fortunate in that my chairman has allowed me to do that. He will support me and make sure I have money to spend on top players, so that we can build on our initial success, hopefully become a team challenging in the middle of the Premiership or for Europe. That's got to be the long term plan for this club. I want international players here, because that would mean they were doing the business week in, week out, playing to the high level demanded of international players. Then, I'm sure, we would have a successful side.

'I took on the challenge of this club because I like the process I hope this club is going to go through. There are clubs like Wimbledon and Southampton – and I don't mean to be disrespectful – who bring in players and then have to sell them to survive. This club have big ambitions. We've got a fantastic new stadium coming along and I've been involved in that, as well, putting in my ideas, and the ideas of my staff, in terms of the facilities and so on. Hopefully I can build a team to match those facilities.

'That's the challenge for me but it's still a long way off. I've achieved nothing yet. The one thing none of us here will do is get carried away because I've seen it all before.'

A knock on the manager's door heralds the arrival of a small boy, wearing a Bryan Robson sweatshirt and bearing Christmas gifts. Chocolate-covered gifts.

'Hiya, pal.'

'That's for you.'

'That's for me? That's very nice of you. I hope you're not trying to get me fat.'

Robson has spent his football life in the Midlands and Manchester, but he was another exile born not too far up the road from here, at Chester-le-Street, and has quickly found a rapport with the locals. 'It is a new environment but I understand the Geordie mentality – you can't really say Geordie here because it's not and they don't like it – the North-East mentality, it's just the same, and these people are just as fanatical as the Newcastle and Sunderland supporters. I know the euphoria you can build up if you are successful in this region. I've got to give them consistent, winning, entertaining performances. If I can do that we'll fill the stadium and the fans will be back.

'Whereas Sunderland and Newcastle have had glory days, Middlesbrough have never quite had that. They have maybe got up into the top League, struggled to survive for one season and gone back down. The fans around this area are fed up of seeing that happen. They want to see this club go on from promotion.'

Robson, recovered from injury after a three-month absence, is content he has a playing contribution to make beyond his 38th birthday, despite the insight into management his recent, single role has given him. 'The injury has given me the opportunity to assess a lot of things around the club, which I maybe wouldn't have been able to do if I'd been playing all the time.

'I'm not thinking of just managing at the moment because I feel I've got as much sorted out in the club as I want at this stage, so that if I am 100 per cent fit I can concentrate on the playing side and leave a lot of the other stuff, off the pitch, to Viv Anderson and John Pickering. We've also got Gordon McQueen in here to take charge of the reserves, so I feel we have a really strong staff. I do think I have plenty more to give yet as a player.'

That does rather beg the question: is there not a part of him that wishes he had stayed at Old Trafford as a player? 'No,' he insists. 'I'm not one to look back. I had a great time at United and it was Alex Ferguson's decision to let me go so that he could bring through some of the younger lads. Whether it was right or wrong, nobody will ever know. But I've no gripes on that.'

Then how about returning to United as manager? 'I know Alex Ferguson really well and it wouldn't surprise me if in another eight years he was still manager of that club, so all the hypothetical talk and speculation is just that. In any case, I might have brought in, say, seven new players here, all 24 or 25, and all of a sudden people are saying, "Hey, Middlesbrough are an exciting young team." And then I might look at the situation and say, "I'm really enjoying the team I'm working with and I want to see them go further." At United you have the Pallisters and the Bruces, and you're going to have to replace them. I just might want to stay here.'

Robson will not be deluded into believing he can quickly bridge that gap. He says: 'People tell me there's not much of a difference between this League and the Premier League, but I'd argue there is. There are some good players in this League, without a doubt, but there is a hell of a difference between the top Premier clubs and the top of this League, and that difference, quite simply, is quality. When you get about halfway down the Premier then yes, you can begin to bring the First Division clubs into play.'

Middlesbrough were so convinced Robson was the man to guide them out of the Endsleigh League they assented to his demand to stay in the Manchester area and take on one of the coaching jobs alongside the England supremo, Terry Venables. To accommodate his manager's domestic requirements, Gibson utilised the club's links with ICI and arranged for Robson to have a seat on the company's executive flight between Manchester and Teesside. But even with that facility, which Robson avails himself of on average once a week, there are those who suspect Captain Marvel may be pushing himself too far this time.

He says: 'I know a lot of people are saying I'm taking on far too much, but I'm learning stuff all the time on the England side of my work, as well as here. It's good for your football education. I enjoy training with the England lads and then in the afternoon Terry, Don Howe and I will sit for maybe four hours, chatting about different aspects of the game.'

Robson is eager to learn. For all his playing experience he is not so arrogant as to believe he is a ready-made manager. 'I made sure I was at least partly prepared by asking established managers about the job. They warned me about the pitfalls and the amount of time you've got to put into it. So although it has meant a big change in my life it's not the sort of life I didn't expect.

'I try to take the good points from all the managers I've worked with, things where I've thought, "I like that." As far as I'm concerned, I couldn't have worked with a better range of managers than I've been lucky enough to. My only club managers were Johnny Giles, Ron Atkinson and Alex Ferguson, and I've worked with Ron Greenwood, Bobby Robson and Terry Venables on the international front. To me, those six would come in the top ten of managers. If you can't learn from them, you're never going to learn.'

Robson has a clause in his contract which would release him from Middlesbrough should his country offer him the ultimate responsibility. Again, however, he plays down the prospect. 'Terry Venables is doing a great job with England. I'm part of that set-up at the moment but I've still got a lot to learn at this level.'

He is, however, satisfied he has found his vocation for the middle part of his life. 'Yes, I do feel management is right for me. Stepping out of the playing aspect into the manager's role, you wonder what sort of reaction you are going to get from the players, but I've had a good response from the players. I've enjoyed it not just in the role here, but even with the England squad, where I've played with a lot of the players and yet I get a good response from them in training, or when we are chatting about a certain tactic. I get a buzz from that.

'You can see if people are listening or whether they are rolling their eyes and not really listening. Whether players take it in and use it is down to them. All any manager can do is try to give players advice on what he thinks is right. Now if the players want to take that in, or they want to let it go out the other ear, is down to them.

'Not every bit of information you give a player is going to be right. I don't think you can be right on everything you say. But as long as you are right on most of the things, and players take it in, you can hope to improve things. Even if that improvement is only five per cent, you're doing a good job for the player, the team and the club. And that, I think, is what management is about.'

Middlesborough won automatic promotion to the Premiership as First Division champions.

CHAPTER 8

The Blunt Blade

Dave Bassett, manager of Sheffield United

The rich variety in our football is reflected in the contrast between Bryan Robson – composed, guarded, deliberate, projecting just the image you would require of an England captain and an England coach – and Dave Bassett, that hyper-active, hyper-talkative, what-you-see-is-what-you-get manager of Sheffield United. Bassett and Bramall Lane seemed an unlikely, even incongruous, alliance back in January 1988. Well, London lad 'Arry, up here in the steel city, with all them Northern folk? As it 'appens, 'Arry and all them Northern folk hit it off big time. They loved him for what he was and most remained loyal when the team were relegated from the Premiership at the end of the 1993/94 season.

Bassett, however, was disillusioned with his employers. Boardroom wrangles and ultimately boardroom changes were symptomatic, he felt, of a club going nowhere. He wanted to go forward, not retreat; he wanted to buy players, not sell; he wanted fulfilment, not frustration. If he saw no signs of United sharing his ambition, he warned, he would have to look elsewhere.

And yet, for all the irritations – the classic seven-year itch? – he turned down the chance to join Leicester City, remained bubbly and approachable, and regenerated some self-belief at the club. Midway through the 1994/95 season United found their First Division feet and were marching in step with the promotion contenders. What's more, they had an FA Cup third round tie at home to Manchester United on the agenda.

It is a cold but bright morning in Sheffield and a few auto graph seekers pursue anything that moves outside the club's smart main stand. Once the targets here were cricketers. This was the Pavilion End when Bramall Lane doubled as a home of Yorkshire CCC. United also used an area back here – euphemistically called the 'Bowling Green' – to train their schoolboy and other amateur players on winter's Tuesday and Thursday evenings. The modest nature of the facilities can be verified by this former schoolboy.

The door to reception swings open and in sweeps Bassett, a 50-year-old with a boyish vitality. I am swept up by the momentum; right, down a corridor, right again and into his office. He is precisely the 'Appy 'Arry you anticipate, but then, given his team's current form, he is entitled to be.

'It's been quite good, brought us up into the top six or seven,' he says, the words instantly flowing. 'But it's been a bit of a climb to get there, which is disappointing because I would have liked to be four or five points better off than we are. We were always battling in the Premier, down at the other end of the table, and although we started the season with optimism the relegation situation was more traumatic for everyone than we realised it would be. It had an effect. It created a dark cloud over the club. I think that's only gone in the last six or eight weeks. Everybody's felt better, everybody's recovered from what happened to us on that last day of last season.

'When the Leicester situation came along, the chairman mentioned they had made an approach and asked was I interested. I had to think, I had to be fair. The club hadn't gone the way I'd wanted in the previous 18 months, since we got to the semi-finals of the FA Cup, and we stayed up. At that time I expected us to go further forward. The board changed to the present board with an EGM and I expected the club to go forward, and they told me they would, but in actual fact we sold Brian Deane and we got relegated.

'During that period we have brought money in, £2 million, but we haven't speculated. It's not gone the way I wanted. We've still got a stand that hasn't been started over the other side – it still looks like a builder's yard – so I feel the club has stagnated during that period. I'm still ambitious. I want a club that can meet my ambitions, and at the moment Sheffield United are not actually doing that. It's all hard work and everything. When we had an opportunity to take that next step forward, the board wasn't able to do it. So I've had to struggle on.

'I thought long and hard about the Leicester situation and I'm not saying that I'd never move. It depends, in the next 18 months, which is the length of my contract: are Sheffield United going to show that they want to go forward, or are they going to stagnate?

If they're going to stagnate, then I'm going to be looking to say, "Well, hold on, this is not quite my cup of tea."

'At the time I felt Leicester wasn't quite right for me or for them. Somehow, something just intuitively, instinctively, wasn't there. That wasn't Leicester's fault, but it was a gut feeling. I might be wrong and we'll never know the answer. I was flattered, but I didn't think it would work.'

Leicester, in any case, represent another relegation struggle. Is he not dismayed the bigger clubs appear to have overlooked him? 'There's been a couple of big clubs that have spoken to me, but the timing's not been right for me. That's the disappointing thing. Going back before Ron Atkinson was there, Aston Villa spoke to me about going there, but it wasn't right to leave Sheffield United. Well, this time, when Ron went, their view was slightly different, so it didn't come up.

'I still believe if Sheffield United can't meet my requirements then perhaps I will get a chance. Joe Royle got his chance with Everton. He kept waiting and I've certainly got ambitions to progress and if your own club can't do it you've got to say perhaps an opportunity will open elsewhere.'

Bassett is gratified to have found sympathy with the club's supporters. He says: 'The fans have been excellent. I've got a good rapport with them. I had one or two letters from fans saying, "We don't blame you if you go. We can see what's happened." They're frustrated and they've demonstrated against the board. They understand but they've also said, "We want you to stay." I think the fans know I've always been fair with them and that I've had to work in very difficult circumstances.

'A lot of them are delighted with the success and the journey we've had in the seven years I've been here. They've had an exciting seven years with me. I think they appreciate what's been achieved. I understand their feelings and frustrations. They had their expectations after that semi-final. I feel just as frustrated as they do.'

It could be, of course, that the bigger clubs are put off by Bassett's 'unsophisticated' style on and off the pitch. He may be the man who lifted Wimbledon from obscurity to the top division and, after an inauspicious spell with Watford, gave the Blades their cutting edge again and kept them among the élite for four seasons, as well as taking them to Wembley for that FA Cup semi-final against Sheffield Wednesday in 1993, but isn't his football a mite too primitive and his tongue too loose?

'People have said that to me. It may well be that I'm a bit Joe Blunt and I say what I feel and sometimes I say the wrong thing. With hindsight, yes, I sometimes think I shouldn't have said this or that, but you are the type of personality you are. You can be a quiet one and get stick and you can be one that says too much. It's very hard to say the right thing all the time. But I always say it with honesty and what I believe in, and I think people know where they stand with me.

'It might frighten one or two people that I might not be quite the IMAGE, I might not be the polished article, as they say, but the one thing I think I am is up front. I'm honest, I admit that I make mistakes. I'm not trying to kid myself I don't. Nobody's ever said to me "You didn't get that job because you're not polished" or "because of your image". Nobody tells you that. It's just an undercurrent type of thing that maybe is there, I don't know. I don't mould myself. I don't worry about anybody else. I'm Dave Bassett, I don't want to be anybody else. I respect other managers and other people, but I am what I am and I'm not going to try to change.

'Admittedly I might sort of think: "Given that same situation I might react in a different way or deal with it differently." That's just a learning process. But Dave Bassett's always going to be . . . a little outspoken. I don't do it deliberately to annoy people or anything, it's how I feel at that particular moment.

'Because of that image, people might think I'm bouncy and enthusiastic all the time, but I have got a serious side and I can be as miserable as the next man. I think I am hard and fair with the players. I think the players respect me and I respect them. As I've always said to my players, I don't necessarily always want them to like me, but if they respect me, that's fair enough. I think most of my players will say I'm up front, I won't say anything behind their backs that I wouldn't say to their faces. I think on the man management side, we get on well.'

But what about the Route One, uncompromising style of play? 'I'm not upset about that image. I was successful with it. To be successful in any walk of life you've got to do things in a different way. Why be criticised? Why should I look back with regret?

I've achieved a lot that a lot of other people haven't done in their lives, and I'm delighted to have done it.

'When I first took over Wimbledon we didn't play Route One football, we played with a sweeper and everything else. But when we were in the Fourth Division nobody took any notice of us. We adapted our football and got different footballers. We worked at it. Unfortunately, people have read about Dave Bassett's teams – long ball, hard players – so they come with preconceived ideas and they report in a biased way. But I've got to live with that.

'I treat them with the contempt they deserve because I think some of them are inane. You just have to get on with it. I can get up in a morning, have a shave and look at myself in the mirror and know what I am. If people start to realise, "Hold on, there's more to this guy than that", then fair enough. They either think that or they don't. You don't end up being a manager for 15 years through luck. You can be a little bit lucky, but you can't be lucky for 15 years.'

I have to take you up on something there, Dave, because I was one of those who upset you with my 'preconceived ideas'. It was at Manchester City, about four years ago. You were talking about the importance of your players having the right attitude and I asked if you were happy with the attitude of your players in that match, when I felt they were over-zealous. In fact, wasn't that the day Vinny Jones got himself booked after four seconds?

'Yeah, Yeah, it might have been. When he got sent off in the second half. We might have been on that day. Listen, I'm not asking for angels. I'm just reading an article by Bryan Robson, saying the game has got to be physical and that we mustn't take that element out of it, and tackling and everything else. I like contact, there should be tackling. If we're not careful the game will become pussy-foot.

'Yes, I mean I'm not saying that all my players are angels all the time, that we do everything right. We don't. Sometimes we do step outside the rules and sometimes the criticism can be justified. Sometimes it's not. But we all end up being tetchy on occasions and sometimes I've been caught in situations where I've thought afterwards perhaps I over-reacted, whereas another day I might have dealt with it differently.

'Now I'm looking for us just to be a football side. I want some long balls, that's for sure. We're not trying to be clever. Every team in the world plays long balls at the right time. You're trying just to get the strengths out of your players. If a short ball's required, or if a ball's needed to be rolled out by the goalkeeper, do it. If it turns out it's not the right ball, then we're doing the wrong things, aren't we? We're playing wrong.

'If a player's trying to pass a little short ball and it ends up being cut out, and they're having an attack on your goal, that was the wrong ball. A long ball would probably have been right. If the long ball ends up going out of touch and they come back at you, that was the wrong ball. I'm trying to get the best out of them and we adapt our system accordingly. I've felt in the last couple of seasons we could have been a bit more direct. We've been a bit too Fancy Dan and it's cost us.

'It's a slow process, getting players to change systems and develop them. Football's a game of evolution. The in-vogue thing might be "Play every ball out of the back and start there", or it might be "Get it up to the front players and play from there". It might be long ball, short ball, get crosses in, play with a sweeper. Football's changing all the time and as a manager or coach you have to be perceptive enough to see that.

'Now we're going through this diamond formation, where everything's slipped through. It's a straight ball played through for a diagonal run or it's a diagonal ball played through for a straight run. Or there's not so many crosses, or it's a little give-and-go. So football goes through all these little stages and I'm sure this will go on for a while and then all of a sudden somebody says, "Let's get back to wingers and crossing the ball." But it's no good saying you'll play wingers if you haven't got them. Like Alf Ramsey in '66. But if you've got Ryan Giggs you don't want him in a diamond shape, you want him wide, to get space, beat people and cross the ball.

'There's no one way that's the right or wrong way to play. I think the best teams are a mixture. There was this thing that if you were a hard-working player you were looked down on. I think you need hard workers, the right attitude, the right composition of your team. You may have a very skilful player who's not a particularly good tackler playing alongside somebody who's a tackler and a runner. That blend is probably right. You can't have 11 Vinny Joneses, you can't have 11 Paul Inces, you can't have 11 Ryan Giggses. It just doesn't work like that.'

Talking of Manchester United got Bassett into a little bother with the double winners' manager, Alex Ferguson, midway through the 1993/94 season. Ferguson felt Bassett, quoted in newspaper articles, was accusing his team of being kickers.

'Alex took it a bit the wrong way,' Bassett insists. 'I was being complimentary. What I said was that Man United weren't a soft touch, that people were talking about what wonderful players they were, but what I said was that they had players like Bryan Robson, Ince, Bruce, Pallister, Hughes and Cantona, and they could look after themselves. I don't knock that at all. I think it's ideal. All the best footballers in the world have that little bit of . . . I just said we'd have a job kicking them off the field because they were not exactly the side you could kick off. I explained afterwards to Alex that I wasn't having a go.

'Now we've got them again in the Cup and it's a hard draw, but we could be away to somebody where there's going to be a small crowd and no television. The club will earn about £250,000 out of this, with Sky and gate receipts and sponsorship, so the chairman's chuffed to pieces with that. And I don't see the Cup as a distraction from the League. People make excuses about that. When you get knocked out of Cups and you're not doing well in the League, you start thinking, "I could do with a lot more games." I can live with the pressure of games, quite easily.'

And when he doesn't have games or training, how does he live his life then? 'My family is my outside life. You sometimes don't give them enough attention. I've got two girls. They've got their horse-riding. We go out to restaurants, or out for walks, that sort of thing, just general family things. I don't mind a game of golf, but I'm not a fanatic. I don't mind going horse-riding. In the summer, we went to Montana, to a cowboy ranch, and I rode all week. There again, I'm not one for riding all the time. Same with a game of tennis.

'Football's my life and it's my hobby, really. Not being funny, but if I was sitting at home and all of a sudden there's a game of football on television, or the chance to go riding or have a game of tennis, I'd rather watch the game of football. It's just the way it is, the way you are. It's been like that since I played as a kid and used to go and watch Chelsea and Fulham. 'Arry was my dad, so that's when I got the nickname "Young 'Arry" and it stuck.

'Ted Drake took me on the ground staff at Chelsea but Tommy Doc (Docherty) bombed me, like Tom does. I have to admit he was right, but it hurt at the time. I played non-League football and then went to Watford, under Ken Furphy. Then I broke my leg, so that sort of finished things. I had an insurance business and a development company. The insurance business still exists, but I'm a dead partner in it. My partner runs that. All I do is turn up for a golf day, the racing day, meet the bank manager and accountant, about four things a year.

'If I wasn't here I'd be a football supporter now. I'd probably be going watching Chelsea or Fulham. I'd probably still be living in that part of the world and I wouldn't be going shopping with the missus, I'd be off to the football.'

You wonder, though, whether he wouldn't be disenchanted with a game widely accused of misusing the money he, as a fan, would be putting into it. Bassett openly admits his club paid Rune Hauge – the Norwegian agent under investigation by tax authorities in his own country and the subject of Premier League inquiries over his role in transfers to English clubs – legitimate fees for bringing two Scandinavian players to Bramall Lane.

'At the end of the day you've got to judge whether the price you are paying for that player is right, and I think what I paid for Roger Nilsen and Jostein Flo was good value. I just think the Norwegians are idiots for not dealing with us directly and getting a better deal for themselves. If a player I want says he's bringing his agent or he's going elsewhere, what do I do, cut my nose off to spite my face? Sometimes the agent is a necessary evil. Whenever I've tried to do a deal with a foreign player an agent has come out of the cupboard, and he's usually from the foreign club. It's the fly-by-night types ripping off players and the game that we don't want. But I don't sympathise with the players there – they've got to learn for themselves.

'Yeah, so there have been a few scandals, allegations of bribes and Merson admitting taking drugs, but this is a nineties situation. You can't hold back the tide of society. Our game's not rotten. You only have to look around the world to see far worse – drugs and match-fixing. We've got nothing on that scale, nothing like that. We've got a good game.'

70

The Blunt Blade

Sheffield United were beaten 2–0 by Manchester United in the third round of the FA Cup, after having Charlie Hartfield sent off in the 14th minute, and slipped out of contention for promotion.

CHAPTER 9

Your Commentary Game Today . . .

Alan Green, BBC radio commentator

Younger fans may be astonished to learn there was a time, not so very long ago, when regular football coverage on television was limited to recorded highlights on BBC's Match of the Day and ITV's Big Match. The only live action came from FA Cup finals and big internationals. The sole medium for League football, as it happened, was BBC radio, and even then all you got was the second half. The chosen match was identified, in melodramatic ritual, after kick-off time. You imagined stampedes to grounds up and down the land at five past three as supporters realised there was no cheap and easy way of following their team that day.

It was generally supposed, of course, that any live commentary would discourage punters from paying at the gate and that over-exposure would seriously affect attendances. How things have changed. The onslaught by television, especially by Sky, has delivered us live League, Cup, representative and any number of other variations in the game, packaged as marathon spectaculars. The BBC and ITV, feeling their backsides suitably kicked, have responded as best they can. Now we have live football three or four days a week. Flick around the channels on a Sunday and the chances are you'll find an Italian match on Four, an Endsleigh League game on ITV and then Premiership fare on Sky. The game succumbed to the multi-million pound offers – again, especially from Sky – and rearranged fixture lists to suit the schedules. And what happened to the gates? They went up.

Football, the culture, has taken on a new dimension and broadcasting has been an integral part of that process. Local radio and club-call services proliferated. At the forefront, however, remained BBC radio, national radio and, under its modern guise, Radio Five, it was able to bring coverage to homes and cars anything up to five days or nights a week. And the most distinctive voice on Radio Five commentaries is that of Alan Green, partly because he is an Ulsterman and partly because he tends to speak his mind rather more than anyone else. His frank assessments have raised eyebrows at Broadcasting House, caused tut-tutting among his peers and incurred the wrath of at least one high-profile manager. Green is unrepentant. He refuses to 'talk-up' a dismal match and has no respect for those who do.

I t is midwinter and mid-season, and Green is particularly busy. Apart from his commentary commitments he is currently hosting the Friday evening *Sportstalk* programme. But then talking comes easily to this chubby-faced enthusiast, and of course he can spare an hour to tell me about himself, his work and his game.

Green was born in Belfast, in 1952, and took a degree in modern history at the city's Queens University. From an early age he had an interest in journalism and earlier still a passion for football.

'My father was a complete lunatic,' he says. 'He supported a team called Linfield and was determined I should do the same. He took me to my first game, he assures me, when I was 18 months old. Linfield were playing Bangor, away, and seemingly I started crying so he took me outside the ground. He will tell anyone – and I've no reason to disbelieve it – that he walked me up and down saying, "Don't you realise the Blues are losing?"

'I remember football earlier than anything else, standing on packed terraces. This was when Linfield would regularly get 25,000–30,000. It sounds ridiculous for an Irish League game, but they did. I remember Newcastle United playing there in the 'Fifties when they first had floodlights at Windsor Park. My regular haunt when Linfield were at home was the Spion Kop, but I went everywhere. In the early 'Sixties they won every trophy, seven of them. I think they beat Glentoran in the County Antrim Shield and I remember crying my eyes out because my father wouldn't let me go on to the pitch. He did, thousands of them did.

'England to me then meant Chelsea Football Club. I think it was just Osgood, all that era. I'm a great one for crying, passion, and I hope that comes through in the commentary, and I remember Chelsea losing to Spurs in the '67 Cup final and I was in a terrible state. The English might find it really odd that people in Northern Ireland can be so passionate towards England.

'I remember the day of the '66 World Cup final, when the equaliser went in, you know, just seconds to go, and we came out of our little council house in Newtownabbey, which is north of Belfast, and we walked in a circle, my father and myself, around the front garden, heads down, thinking, "We'll never do it now." We were devastated. People were all out in their gardens, shouting, "We're going to lose it now."

'When I first came to England I didn't know how to get to Anfield or Old Trafford, these places were overwhelming to me. They were images I saw on TV or heard of on radio, not something I could actually touch. I feel like a privileged punter now. I'd like to think I'm someone who's feeling the same emotions about the game as the guy who has had to pay his money. The difference is I've got a microphone which, through experience, doesn't intimidate me. It's like a friend and I can just voice what I'm thinking and what he might be thinking and transmit that to those who can't be there.'

Green began his journalistic career in a less privileged role, working as a copy boy at the *Belfast Telegraph* during school holidays. 'That was shoving things up shoots and "Can you open this beer on the edge of the cabinet for me?" My sole ambition was to be a news reporter on the *Belfast Telegraph*. There was no journalistic connection in the family. My father was an overlooker in a mill. It was my careers officer at university who suggested I apply for the BBC news training scheme.'

It was the first of many unscheduled turns in Green's career. 'I really thought this was way beyond me, but I was offered it so I started with the BBC, 20 years ago. They take a certain number of graduates a year to train as broadcasting journalists, who are unsullied by newspaper techniques. I felt completely overwhelmed. This was Broadcasting House, in London, and every day on the way to the news training office you pass the *World At One* offices, to the left the *World This Weekend*. It was just mind-blowing. And all the others on the course – there were seven of us – were Oxbridge graduates and I felt completely inadequate. But things worked out all right.

'At that time I had only one interest and that was to be editor of the *Nine O'Clock News*. I wanted to run it, not present it, and I still feel more strongly, I'm still more critical, about how television news is presented than anything that happens in sports journalism. I feel I'm a journalist first and a sports journalist second. I did a series of attachments around the BBC, local radio, regional television news rooms, that kind of thing, and I diverted into sport.

'I was a television news reporter in Belfast, didn't like the atmosphere, and got a job on a weekly sports magazine programme. Then they pushed me into commentary because they had nobody else. I did the Irish Cup final for television and found it pretty pathetic. Didn't sleep the night before, certainly didn't sleep the night after, thinking how bad it was. There weren't that many commentaries to do, maybe eight or nine a year, European Cup matches involving Irish League teams or Northern Ireland games. But you get to know a little bit about it and I improved.

'I reached the stage in Belfast where I thought that was it, I couldn't really go much further and I'd be doing this for the next 30 years. There were jobs in radio sport in London and I applied for them. They'd basically already been allocated but I was offered a job in Manchester. I said "no" because if I was going to make the break and bring my wife anywhere it would be to London because logically that's where I'd like to end up.

'Anyway, I was talked into Manchester. I started essentially as the reporter-feature maker for Northern football and again commentary wasn't even on the horizon. Except that just before I made the move to Manchester the Head of Sport in Northern Ireland said to me. "By the way, your first commentary is on the 28th of February, England against Northern Ireland at Wembley." I said, "What are you talking about?" and he said they wanted me to do some radio commentary. I said I couldn't do radio commentary, but it had been sorted and I had to do it.

'Robson scored after less than a minute and I was sweating. There I was working with a legend for me, Peter Jones, and Ron Greenwood summarising. I felt so out of my depth. I barely recognised . . . well, I knew it was Robson and got it out, but I thought it was awful, absolutely awful, and I cringed. I was treating it like a television commentary – "I'm not telling you what's happening here, you can see it for yourself." That first experience of radio commentary, 12 years ago, told me I couldn't do it. Other people persuaded me to carry on. This is very hard to take for the young boys who write to me because they automatically assume I had that ambition, but I didn't. It just happened.'

Green's promotion to senior status in the commentary team came in tragic circumstances. It followed the death of that broadcasting 'legend', Peter Jones. 'No-one could touch Jonesy,' his apprentice says. 'He would do all the main commentaries and remember we did relatively few games then. You're talking about Saturday games, Wednesday night games, internationals, that's it. Not this five or six days a week business that we go through now.

'So, when Jonesy was doing all these big games it left very few opportunities for the third and fourth strings, people like myself and Mike Ingham. We would get, if we were lucky, a League Cup replay that Jonesy didn't fancy. But there was no resentment at all, because Jonesy was the best and that was just the way of life. We would all do more as the commentaries increased, but we were still missing out on the big ones.

'When Jonesy died in 1990, on the day of the Boat Race, I was doing commentary at Wolves. They were playing Leeds and they'd just built their new stand. Martin Chivers was summarising. I was disturbed that day because we seemed to be so far from the pitch and I couldn't really make out the players, a nightmare to do a commentary. Peter was at the Boat Race and it was Martin who noticed it first. "I think there's something wrong with Peter," he said. Peter was an old friend of his and he said, "Peter doesn't sound great." Then Peter didn't pick up a link and we thought, "What is this?"

'We tried to buzz the studio with an electronic device we have but they said they were busy. Eventually they told us Jonesy had collapsed on the towpath but they didn't know what condition he was in. It was announced on television that night that he had collapsed. I think he died in the early hours of Sunday morning.

'That very day the Head of Sport rang me and said, "Look, unfortunately we've got to think business." That week or a couple of weeks later I was due to go over to the World Snooker, which I'd covered for eight or nine years straight, but they said they'd got to pull me off it, I'd got to go full-time football commentary, and that's how it was. It's terrible because it's "dead men's shoes".'

Green prepares for his work by simply soaking up the football flooding our lives. 'I can't afford to miss anything that's on, say, Sky. I don't actually like Sky's approach but I need that input. Because I see so much football and because so much of it happens to be at the top level, I shouldn't have to prepare that much to go and do, for example, Newcastle and Manchester City. If I don't know these teams I shouldn't be doing it. But on FA Cup third round day I'll be doing Birmingham and Liverpool. Well, I don't need to know about

Liverpool but I've never seen Birmingham play live, so I'm going to have to make sure I know that side.'

So what is it about Sky's approach he does not like?

'It isn't doing my career prospects any good but even if anybody in television sport or satellite television thought I was any good, they wouldn't take me on, because I'm not going to say things they want me to say. If a game is bad I'm just going to call it that way. That may seem unfair on commentators in television and on satellite I respect, but I think there are pressures on them. We're talking about contracts here.

'If, for example, commentator A, working for Channel A, has seen a lot of drivel in terms of the games he's watching, he's reflecting that, but he doesn't have to go too far because the viewers can see it for themselves. But if he's not trying to bluff the viewer then the sponsors, the people who allow Channel A to get the contract, are going to say, "Hold on a second, they're not selling our product the way we want them to sell it." So there are pressures there that I don't have to work under and I appreciate that.

'I certainly like to be provocative, that's true, but that's inbuilt. If you are a punter and you see an incident in the penalty area you are going to have a view on it. I see my role beyond just describing. It's not something that is generally liked, even within my own department. There are times when the head of department will say, "I thought you went a little bit over the top there." On the other hand, my current head of department is of a view that if he said to me, "I want you to commentate without attitude", or, "I want you to commentate without letting your feelings come across", he knows he would ruin me as a commentator. So, if he feels I've gone over the top he'll say so quietly and I'll take it on board.

'I don't get much reaction from players. I'm not sure how many of them listen to the radio. Or maybe they just don't get offended. Managers do sometimes. Alex Ferguson and I simply do not have a relationship. I don't think it was anything specific. I remember very well the day Alex got the job at Old Trafford. I'd known him at Aberdeen and I went to interview him and we were standing on the touchline looking at the floodlights. It wasn't quite the stadium it is now but it's always had something special. I said, "Do you realise what you are taking on here?" He was looking sort of starry-eyed and I felt a great empathy with him at the time. I'd come across the sea and it dazzled me. Stadia like that still dazzle me. Alex was looking and saying, "Isn't this fantastic?"

'I thought at that stage we were going to get on well, but I did feel he came to England paranoid about Merseyside, absolutely paranoid. I think it was a paranoia born in his own feelings when he was manager of Aberdeen and he was looking at Rangers and Celtic when they were dominating everything. He was coming to a scene at Manchester where Ron Atkinson had basically got the sack because he couldn't match Liverpool and Everton. Fergie had to do that and I think he felt this was the big bugbear that he had to get rid of so he had this inbuilt paranoia.

'Secondly, and like so many people, he misunderstood my enthusiasm for good football as support for a particular side. Over the years I've had letters claiming I supported X, Y and Z, but what it actually boils down to is that I praised X, Y and Z because they played good football. So, if you praise teams playing well and winning, you're supporting them. It's just not true. But since Liverpool were winning everything in sight, and I praised them, Fergie misinterpreted that and labelled me a Liverpool fan.

'There were a couple of scenes, one at Anfield, during the period when he had a row with Kenny Dalglish. He had a major scene with me that day, accusing me of being a Liverpool fan and saying he wouldn't talk to me, and I told him he was crazy. He's never got over that. I think he has an appalling attitude towards me. In a perverse way it's flattering because why should the manager of the biggest club in the country give two damns what I say? But he appears to care about it and to care to such a degree that he is forever slagging me off, publicly and privately, and it means, frankly, that from a situation where I quite liked the man I now have no time for him on a personal level.

'On a professional level, yes, but I think the key to the reason why we shall never be friends is that I don't wear a Manchester United scarf. I've no reason to. I'm not a sycophant like so many members of the national press. I continue to say what I think even if I know he's not going to like it. I criticised him for leaving Bruce out against Barcelona at Old Trafford, for leaving Schmeichel out in Barcelona. Well, he wouldn't have liked that but it wouldn't change what I said. If he gets worked up about it, too bad.'

Coping with a hostile manager is one thing. Hillsborough, 1989, was quite another. Green's recollections are as moving as they are graphic.

'I was with Peter Jones and I loved the days when FA Cup semi-finals were on Saturdays, kicking off at three o'clock and at 20 minutes to five you knew who was going to be at Wembley. What really bugs me about television and satellites, they're taking away so many traditions that we love, like the FA Cup draw at lunchtime on Monday, that whole business. I'm a great traditionalist.

'Anyway, at the start of the game [*Liverpool v Nottingham Forest*] we'd no idea what was happening. I saw Grobbelaar making gestures towards something at the Leppings Lane end. The game's been stopped at seven minutes past three and even then we don't have a clue what's going on. Jonesy is the main commentator and he had to stay up and talk in our commentary position at Hillsborough so I said I'd go down to the dressing-room to see what was going on. And then the whole thing unfolded and the whole day just got worse.

'I remember specific times in the day. I befriended this policeman because no information was coming out and we were getting calls from people wanting to know what was happening, some saying they had relatives there. I shouted to this cop, "We're talking about people dying in there, we've got to have a telephone number." He did get a number. I remember interviewing Graham Kelly at 4.20 and he was crying. It just went on and on. I was bottling up my emotions. I was too busy working. I was conscious, of course, of what was going on, that bodies were being taken over to the gym in the far corner. *Sports Report* was over and there was nothing I could do.

'Radio news had sent up their reporters. It had become a news story. Jonesy had to get the train back to London and it was the opening day of the Snooker World Championship in Sheffield and my commitment was to go on from the semi-final and do that evening's snooker at The Crucible. So I took Jonesy to the railway station and we were both crying in the car. I dropped him off and drove to The Crucible. I parked in the NCP, walked through the doors and I think everything had just built up.

'I was about to walk into the press room and walked straight into Steve Acteson, who was then the Press Association's snooker correspondent [*now a sports reporter on the* Today *newspaper*] and basically fell into his arms. He literally dragged me to the gents. I'm in there crying my eyes out and Tony Knowles is in there and he knows what's happened. Tony had a reputation for being this big, good-looking, not very bright lad, but he was really concerned about me and the whole day. And he was playing that evening. The next day he lost but he came to see how I was. Never forget that. It was a terrible week and I was just on auto-pilot. I was describing snooker but not watching it. That was definitely my worst experience.

'The following Saturday I was still at the snooker but London said they needed me to go to Bramall Lane because it was the first game in Sheffield after the tragedy. I didn't want to do it and they gave me 24 hours to think about it, and in the end I knew I had to do it – as much for myself as anything else. I was sitting in the car outside Bramall Lane at midday and the South Yorkshire police had gathered. I remember these policemen walking down, laughing and joking. I wasn't certain what had happened at Hillsborough but I felt the police had had a very negative role in what had happened and I thought some of those guys must have been at Hillsborough last Saturday, how can they be laughing and joking?

'I went into the ground and at seven minutes past three the bells tolled in Sheffield. I was standing at the back of the press box just quivering, crying my eyes out. It was just devastating.

'I know it sounds corny and clichéd, but I still think of Hillsborough. But in terms of crying about it, in terms of dissolving, it ended the day of the Cup final. I couldn't bear to be in our commentary position when Gerry Marsden was singing *You'll Never Walk Alone*. I had to leave and stand at the back. I must sound like a right weepie but I just couldn't handle it. I drove home from Wembley that night and got back in time to watch *Match of the Day* and they had a sort of re-cap of the season, which of course involved Hillsborough, and I just fell apart. But I haven't cried about it since. I think that was the end.'

Green did, however, handle his job, as he and his fellow professionals have to, but if Hillsborough marked the deepest trough in his career there have been emotional highs to sustain the soul. 'Just being at big games and being really pleased about something that has happened,' he says. Just like a fan. Unlike a fan, he must maintain a level of impartiality and objectivity.

'In an England game one of the producers rightly pulled me up for using the term "we" and I've never forgotten it. When I'm commentating on an England game I want England to win. I'd be crazy not to. Professionally, I need England to win. They are an integral part of my career. I want every English club to do well in Europe, even if personally I might not care too much about them. But no, I don't think I'm jingoistic.'

Big matches do not necessarily mean the best working conditions, as Green illustrates with almost masochistic relish.

'People do have this image that it's all bloody glamour, best seats in the house, and frequently we do have the best seats in the house. The position at Old Trafford is magnificent. But at Innsbruck, for a European match against Liverpool, our commentary position was on top of a hamburger stall. The stench was appalling.

'The worst of all was when United were playing Torpedo Moscow, defending the Cup-Winners' Cup. It's an afternoon kick-off in Moscow, belting down with rain and it's freezing cold. We'd been to the ground, a pretty poor ground, the day before and we thought we had this little enclosed commentary booth. Our bus got waylaid and, 35 minutes from going on air, I'm running up to the commentary position when the producer shouts at me to follow him. He's on the running track. We walk down to the corner flag and there's a single-decker bus.

'He said, "Don't say anything, I'd no choice. This is where we've got to do the commentary from." Jimmy Armfield is behind me and we step on to this bus and it's like something you imagine from the Second World War. There's a little slot, about nine inches, with a sliding window and the idea is that I do the commentary looking out of this gap. You do one of two things: you either throw a tantrum like a prima donna and say you're not doing it or you laugh and get on with it. So I laughed and got on with it, and made it the centre-piece of the commentary.'

The wonderful bonus for listeners to live radio is the inevitable smack of pundit/expert on banana skin and they do not have to wait for one of those out-take specials to enjoy it. There it is, fresh on the airwaves. The clanger is an occupational hazard for a broadcaster.

'A Crystal Palace match at Selhurst Park,' Green remembers with lingering disbelief. 'I think I gave the goal to Mark Bright and as I did so the producer is shaking his head and I'm looking along wondering what I've done wrong. Then the summariser came in and said it was actually Geoff Thomas. Now there's not a racist bone in my body but I literally got a black player and a white player mixed up. Don't know how I did it, but we all make mistakes. There are too many games not to make mistakes. If you don't know, say so. I think that's as much a part of my commentary as being blunt, forthright – the fact that I don't know just what I am going to say or I don't mind making an ass of myself.

'I think people listening like that. They like you to be human. That reflects in the letters I get. They like the personal thing. Lots of people I work with don't like it. People I work with have recently been saying, "You say far too much in your commentary, leave it to the summariser." If all the summarisers had something to say I probably wouldn't say anything, or at least be less inclined to. But I am exactly the same off air as I am on it. I am the same opinionated, far too opinionated, Irishman. I am definitely conscious of the cult thing. The danger is you begin to believe it as opposed to just getting on with it.

'I think the TV channels should be more opinionated, definitely. I think some of them are. I'm a great Barry Davies fan. I think Barry's a wonderful commentator. I like the way he's not afraid to say things. There aren't that many more. I don't like leaning on statistics. I just think they are a crutch. I think you should have enough to say about the game, even if it's bad. You should have the confidence to get on with it.

'It's not a matter of my having TV aspirations now – I don't think it will happen and I don't really give it any thought. I make quite a few enemies. I have enemies in television and I know there are certain parts of television I'll never get near until people leave. It's not the most highly paid job, radio. There's a bit of envy and resentment on my part. I envy the television boys who earn a lot of money, particularly in cases where I feel they are not particularly good at it. Certainly satellite.

'I envy them and I also resent it because there's a perception of me, of having a glamour job and earning lots of money, that I've got it made. I wish it was true but it's not. It's no secret I never clear up my overdraft. In my view I have a very average salary and I drive a bog-standard company car which is given to me only because the BBC saves money that way.'

The burden of that envy can be as nothing compared with the physical disorder Green has to live and work with.

'I've been diabetic for 30 years. I don't think it's a handicap, it's just something I live with. I take injections in the oddest places. Like in Barcelona, for the United game. We had these glass commentary booths, I looked around to make sure no-one was watching me with the syringe and the insulin and did what had to be done. Anyone who might have seen me must have thought I was shooting something really serious. I suppose I don't look after my diabetes as well as I should but it's just part of a life pattern. It's not possible to be strict. There have been times when I haven't felt well, but it's never stopped me doing a commentary in radio sport, which is 13 years.

'I raised the subject with Gary Mabbutt once, just on the lines of saying, "By the way, Gary, I'm a diabetic too and I'm interested to know how you handle it." I think someone like Gary is bound to have problems because of the intensity of physical effort. If I spend an hour and a half bloody shopping I'm looking for sugar to get my level up, so what it must be like playing 90 minutes of football at the highest level I can't begin to imagine. I think he eats a lot of Mars bars.'

Green lives with his wife, Brenda, and two children, Sarah and Simon, at Macclesfield, Cheshire. True to family tradition, Simon has become indoctrinated in the football culture. Linfield fan? Chelsea, maybe? Er, no.

'He's a lunatic Man United fan and this is not something his father approves of. I'm just trying to coach him in the beauty of the game generally rather than the beauty of a club, particularly one whose manager hates my guts. Simon has actually been known to say, when Fergie has appeared on television, "That's the man who hates my dad." But it hasn't stopped him loving the club and on days off I've actually taken him to Old Trafford. Is this something Fergie should know about?

'To be honest there isn't much spare time for anything outside the job. It's incredibly destructive, the sort of life we lead. Most weekends are cluttered, and most days now. They are trying to tie us down to three commentaries a week. At the last European Championship I did seven games in nine days, in different cities. I do between 130 and 140 commentaries a season. The only time I have for any other work, apart from this current stint on *Sportstalk*, is for golf. I'm looking forward to the PGA, Wentworth, the Open and the Ryder Cup. I've done the Ryder Cup since 1985.

'I enjoy golf not just for the change of pace but the change of people. There are a lot of people in football I get on with very well, a lot of people I respect, but in terms of PR it's a pathetic sport. The players have a lot to learn, whereas in golf, almost without exception, the players know the benefit of getting on with the media, of explaining to them. That's not to say you don't have the occasional clash – say Nick Faldo with the written press – but they see the need to go and explain.

'It was interesting to hear Fergie after the Galatasaray game at Old Trafford. He said something on the lines that the media didn't understand his tactics. Well, there's a simple answer to that: just explain them. To be fair, in golf it's not the same pressure. There's not the same intensity of interest. But it's a delight to be working with people you can get on with. Most footballers I wouldn't dream of socialising with. But I love the game and it's not going to take me away from it. I'm not going to make friends but it's the truth: they want to gripe, they think you're out to get them and it's absolute drivel.

'People can criticise me and some of the criticism I won't like but so what? All I can say is that if I am critical of a footballer or a team, or of a situation, it's honest. There'll be times when I get it wrong but it's my honest opinion and that's all I ask them to accept, but most of them can't accept that because they are paranoid about criticism. When I stop doing this in 20 years it won't have changed. Pressure is just going to go up.

'Will I change? No, I don't think so. When I first went to Manchester Don Mosey was sort of king there. He was a bit like me and I thought of him as, in quotes, "a bitter old man". You know, pungent views. I sometimes think now there is a danger I'm going to be a bitter old man. Maybe not bitter but I don't see the pungency of my views changing. No matter how critical I am, I always take something positive from a game, or something to laugh about.

'An incident in Gothenburg: Jimmy Armfield thought I was too hard on Man United. I told him to read the papers the following morning. Anyway, I was doing my after-match piece, which was pretty damning, and I looked up and there were four United punters standing in front of me. They'd paid hundreds of pounds to get to Gothenburg and I was wondering what they were going to say. What they said was, "You're absolutely right, weren't they pathetic? What are we doing paying out all our money for this?"'

Even conversation with Green is an emotional roller-coaster. We hurtle up and down because that is the way he is, and he is candid enough to reveal himself the way he is. It would, however, be unfair and misrepresentative to linger in depths of despair. He is, essentially, an up-beat character in love with sport and grateful for the opportunity to involve himself in momentous sporting occasions.

'In great stadiums like Milan and Barcelona I've looked around and I've thought, "Hey, someone's paying you to be here, however pitiful you may think the money might be, and you've got this great scene and you are able to commentate on the sport you love." There can't be much better than that. If I'm really passionate about a goal and I know it's important, like Lineker equalising against Germany in the World Cup, in Turin, the tears are there. I'm still describing the goal thinking, "This is so bloody important." That's just great.

'A little story about that to show what it can mean to a lot of people: The Stones were playing at Wembley that night and there were about 70,000 at the concert, and in the middle of a number Mick Jagger stops because there is a huge roar around Wembley. It didn't relate to anything he was doing on stage and he looked around as if to say, "What's going on?" Then he was told Lineker had equalised. People had gone to that concert with their transistor radios, and they've reacted to that moment I was lucky enough to commentate on.

'I once asked Mick Jagger for his autograph on behalf of Mike Ingham at Loftus Road. I also met Phil Collins and the funny thing is he knew me through commentary. Here I am, looking at this guy and I'm thinking he's got everything I wish I had and he's talking football to me and he's heard me on the radio, which is crazy. Despite my piddling salary!'

CHAPTER 10

Rich Man, Poor Man

Jürgen Klinsmann, formerly of Tottenham Hotspur and Germany, and Gary Bennett, formerly of Wrexham

Nothing embraces and celebrates the principle of democracy in football like the FA Cup. It is the competition open to the masses, marvelled at and envied around the world. The mighty and the humble, rich and poor are at the mercy of the 'one-off' occasion that fuses fantasy and reality. Two of the unlikely stars featured in the story of the 1994–95 trail to Wembley were Jurgen Klinsmann and Gary Bennett, strikers from opposite ends of the game's spectrum.

Klinsmann had coveted from afar the chance to acquaint himself with a sporting institution. A World Cup winner with Germany and a multi-lingual Eurocrat, Klinsmann joined Tottenham Hotspur in the summer of 1994 for a £2 million fee and a reported £23,000 a week, yet was no nearer a shot at that most enduring of prizes. Spurs, charged over financial irregularities, had been deducted 12 Premiership points (later reduced to six) and thrown out of the FA Cup for the coming season.

An incident in an FA Cup tie in 1987 almost distanced Bennett from any fraternisation in the glory game. He was condemned for the challenge which broke an opponent's leg and spent what should have been the best years of his career in a kind of purgatory. Vilified, ostracised and victimised by many of his peers, he endeavoured to eke out a living from the game despite the 'bad boy' mantle and the reluctance of potential employers. He signed for Wrexham from Chester on a free transfer in 1992 after a dispute over pay. He had been offered a rise of £5 a week.

A distinctive, high-stepping silhouette appears on a foggy, frosted backdrop as a reticent sun ventures over Spurs' Mill Hill training ground in North London. Soon we can make out the floppy, golden hair. And black gloves. Could only be a foreign player wearing gloves. Everything else about Klinsmann is unobtrusive. Others appear more at ease and more expressive in every sense on the frozen pitches. Nick Barmby is terrific. So is Teddy Sheringham. He's also the one with the rabbit.

Klinsmann is quickly on his way across the fields and back to the dressing-room at the end of the session. He is one of the first in his civvies, too, but his work schedule is by no means over. He stands out in the cold recording an interview for German television, then obliges a local radio man. 'It's freezing. Let's go and have a cup of tea,' he says, beckoning me towards a hut in the corner of the grounds.

Klinsmann has taken to a few English traditions as the English game has taken to him. Sure, he had talent, but did we really need HIM? Wasn't he the player who turned diving into an art form? He addressed that matter with his opening public remarks as a Tottenham player, inquiring where he might find the nearest diving school. He followed up with celebratory dives after his first goals for his new club, home and away. Smart guy.

He has charmed the cynicism from all of us. He has won not only the affections of the Spurs' supporters but also the admiration of football followers across the land with consistently high standards of performance, boundless enthusiasm and a demeanour unsullied by conceit, suspicion or hang-ups. He is a class act on and off the field, articulate and diplomatic in four languages, an example to professional sportsmen everywhere.

The son of a Stuttgart baker, he developed a taste for football and travel, journeying from his home city club to Internazionale of Milan and Monaco. Without making a song and dance about it, he has supported Greenpeace, other environmental campaigns and a variety of charities. He is similarly generous with his time. He does not demand fees for interviews, but then he does not have an agent. He can afford to be philanthropic and admits as much. He could also afford any or even all the flash cars driven by his team-mates. Sponsors would love him to parade their luxury on wheels. Instead he drives around in his beloved old VW Beetle. In central London he also uses the underground. 'Yes, I use the tube,' he says, 'it's wonderful.' In order to enjoy the full cosmopolitan delights of the city, he and his American girlfriend moved into a flat near Regent's

Park rather than settle for the regimental modern five-bed detached in suburbia. Klinsmann is engagingly different, his own man in any environment.

Come mid-season, he found himself confronting a bewilderingly different football scenario. Early success gave way to poor results and the Spurs manager, Osvaldo Ardiles, gave way to Gerry Francis. He reorganised the team, particularly its defence, and Spurs climbed the Premiership table again. What's more, the club's chairman, Alan Sugar, successfully contested the FA's disciplinary measures at an independent tribunal. Those six League points were restored and so was the club's place in the FA Cup. Suddenly there was talk of Wembley and Europe. Klinsmann was in a winter wonderland that strained even his craving for adventure.

Klinsmann recalls with a smile (or is it a shudder?): 'The first thing Alan Sugar said to me was, "Before you consider Tottenham, we are in big trouble." He was straightforward, explaining about the points and being out of the FA Cup.'

Then why Spurs, a club on the threshold of crisis? Why England? He was just 30, fresh from another outstanding series of World Cup performances, there must have been other, more enticing propositions?

'I had three options,' he says. 'Genoa, in Italy, Atletico Madrid, in Spain, and Tottenham. Italy is nothing new for me. I would be going back to a very good Championship, but you wouldn't learn anything. Atletico was maybe not my big wish. If you talk about Real Madrid or Barcelona, this is different, but Atletico is not one of the biggest clubs.

'Tottenham meant to me a very traditional club, with fans who follow them to the away games, creating a good atmosphere everywhere. It meant England, a totally different Championship, a very exciting one. And it meant living in London, an international city. I wanted to be part of the city and I had to make up my mind in a couple of days. Tottenham, English football – it was the kind of challenge I wanted.

'They were building a team for the future, a quality team. They were ambitious. So I said, "Okay, this handicap we have to accept, but six points is only two victories. [*He actually says victory but he gets enough ribbing about that from his team-mates.*] We can make that. And the FA Cup, we have to live with that decision."

'I was surprised and a little hurt to hear these stories about my diving. The media in Germany took up the stories that the papers had here and reacted by saying, "What are they doing to our Klinsmann?" I wondered what was going on and didn't know what to do. I have a friend in Nice who lived in England five or six years and he said, "They want to provoke you. It's a test, to find out how you react. You have only one chance, you have to make a joke out of it. This is English humour."

'I said I could make plenty jokes. No problem at all. So I did this joke about the diving school. The diving after the first two goals was not my idea, it was Teddy Sheringham's idea. He said I had to do it and the whole team would. Suddenly it turned things totally.

'We started very well, and I thought the six points would not be a problem any more. But then suddenly we struggled, defensively, not because we were not organised enough, which a lot of people said, or because we had tactical problems. We had problems defensively because we made too many mistakes individually. That's why we conceded so many goals.

'Then we changed the manager and Gerry Francis took over. He said first of all he wanted to solve these individual problems. He had his own philosophy and his own thoughts about training the team and things have gone better. I was sorry for Ossie, but over ten or 12 years I have had so many different managers. As a player you know that when there is a new manager a couple of things will change. Gerry Francis, for example, does a running session at the beginning of the week, usually on Tuesday. It is hard physical work. But you do your work. It's your job.

'English training is different because here you work with the whole squad, about 30 or 35 players together, and this is really new for me. I never saw such big squads before. In every team I was with before we had a squad of 18 or 20 players – at Monaco, Inter Milan or Stuttgart. In Italy you have a youth team behind and at Stuttgart a reserve team participates in the second or third division. They have their own programme, their own training, totally independent of the professionals.

'The style of football is also different in England. It's much faster than in Italy or France. For sure, the competitive side was one of the attractions. They have the mentality here that they always go for it. They just try to win, even when they play away games. In Italy or France, there is the attitude sometimes that a point is enough. They think more tactically.'

For all its attractions, some of English football's finest have been found wanting in Europe. Blackburn, Manchester United, Newcastle United and Aston Villa all made early departures from the Continental arena.

'It's a question of experience,' Klinsmann suggests. 'It was a big problem for English clubs that they could not play in European competition for many years. With more experience, Newcastle and Aston Villa would not have lost the way they did. Teams from Italy, especially, understand what is required, they think one step ahead. But quality-wise, there is no difference. You could see that with Newcastle and Aston Villa.

'I am really happy with the quality and technique in this country. But when you play very fast, it's normal that you make mistakes. If you take out the speed it's easier to play. It means you can stop the ball, you look and you pass. When you play fast you have to know where you want to pass the ball before you have it. That means you make more mistakes.

'I would say on some occasions you should be more controlled and adapt to the European requirements. You can see that over the years German teams have learned that. In Germany they also play a very fast, open game, but when they play in the European Cup games they know they have to be careful. Maybe just to win 1–0 is already a good result at home. At least you don't concede a goal. In Italy the manager may not be upset if you draw 0–0 at home because he believes you are going to score one goal away. When we won the UEFA Cup with Inter it was this kind of result that took us through to the final.

'I think it can only help the English game to have foreign players here and I do not say that because I am foreign. Look at the Italian League. Over the last ten or 12 years it has been the number one League because it has had foreigners. They are not so blind that they cannot see that. It has been the number one because of players like Maradona, Careca, Van Basten, Rijkaard, Matthaus and so on. At the same time I learn from the English style, in terms of going the whole 90 minutes, always fighting. If you are losing but the people see you are doing your best they stand up and clap their hands. You don't have this kind of mentality in Germany.

'I think, though, there are too many games in England and it's a good step to reduce the Premier League to 20 teams, and then to 18 would be good, especially when you have two Cup competitions. Alex Ferguson was right to play his younger players for Manchester United in the Coca Cola Cup. It makes sense. To play four games in eight days at Christmas does not make sense. It can be a struggle for teams with small squads. You can only lose quality with so many games. To do well in Europe you have to look after your players.'

The lean and agile Klinsmann has learned to look after himself in both his professional life and his private life. Moving away from Germany spared him the pressures encountered by tennis stars Boris Becker and Steffi Graf, and coming to London has given him the cover to experience a relatively normal existence.

He says: 'I never had the problem of being built up quickly and then knocked down. For me popularity came very slowly. And then it helped to be away from Germany. They could not push me down because they could not build me up. I know how to handle situations. For example, my private life is mine. Nobody comes into my apartment and takes photographs because this is the last piece of privacy I have. I can't do anything if they wait for me in the street and take pictures of me with my girlfriend, or whatever, but I don't talk about my privacy because then I would have given it away. In Germany they try to get me to bring my girlfriend on to a TV show. I know they just want to kick around my privacy. It's the same with magazines.

'London helps because it's such a big place, seven million people. They don't care. Okay, they recognise me but never give me problems. They say hello or a little boy asks for an autograph. It's a pleasure to give him a smile.

'I am comfortable with people and the media until a certain point. When I feel it is getting too much, and start to feel uncomfortable, then I stop it. When it's a relaxed atmosphere, not too much tension, it's no problem, I can handle it. In Milan I couldn't walk around the centre in the middle of the day. I did it once and it became crazy. You get a crowd and it gets out of control. In the evening it was different. I could go to nice coffee bars and restaurants, and talk to people, and have no problem.

'These experiences are targets for me just as playing achievements are. I missed out on student life but I have learned so many things since I started playing. Probably when I stop playing I will look back and say, "It doesn't matter if you scored 20 or 30 goals a season, but that you learned different languages, you knew how to handle different mentalities. This is something you can be proud of."

'I don't know what I will do because I don't know where I will live when I stop playing. I love Stuttgart because my family and most of my friends are there. I also had a wonderful time in Italy and bought a little house on Lake Como. I also made a lot of friends there and my Italian is better than my English. I could stay longer in England but I have enough experience in this business to know you can't plan anything. Contracts don't mean anything, only a certain financial guarantee.

'I don't think I will become a manager. I get my own motivation out of myself and don't need someone telling me, "Come on, come on." I would have problems dealing with adults every day, telling them how they have to prepare for games and what they have to do on the pitch. For sure I will play until the European Championships in '96 and then I will decide year by year. I still want to win competitions – the European Championship with Germany, and before that maybe the FA Cup with Tottenham.

'There is no doubt that in England the Cup is kind of special. Germany took over this kind of mentality but in Italy, for instance, the Cup is not that important. Only for a place in Europe. To be in the FA Cup now is a nice bonus for me. Really nice.'

Klinsmann and Tottenham set out on the odyssey that was not supposed to happen against Altrincham, opponents he confesses are a mystery to him. 'To be honest, I don't know where Altrincham is. I think they are in the Third Division, right?'

Not quite. The Conference, actually. And Altrincham is in Greater Manchester. He does, though, have an idea what to expect.

Respectfully, he continues: 'Over the years I have had a lot of experience in Cup competitions against lower division teams, and we have always struggled. We maybe go on to win five or six-nil, but before you score the first goal you always struggle. So you have to take these games very seriously and that is how we have to take this game against Altrincham.

'Just to think of Wembley is exciting. When I came to England I looked for the special games, in stadiums I always wanted to play in. Anfield was one, Old Trafford another. But there could be nothing better than to finish the season at Wembley, in the FA Cup final.'

The sky above the Racecourse Ground, home of Wrexham Football Club, is the hue of slate gouged from the mountains of Snowdonia. The wind is pummelling the stands; the rain will doubtless follow. They do not torment themselves with dreams of Wembley in these parts, even if they have seen off Arsenal here and more recently gave an honourable account of themselves against Coventry City in the Coca Cola Cup.

Normally the conversation centres on games against Crewe and Shrewsbury and Brentford. It must be difficult to get out of the routine. Two supporters, savouring the local brew in the club bar, are pursuing a familiar theme – the raw deal afforded travelling fans. 'I couldn't get half price for my little one there,' moans one. 'Chesterfield was the best,' he resumes, putting down his glass.

'Did you get half price there?' asks his pal.

'No, no half price, but the fellow on the turnstile there says, "Lift the little one over".'

We are, you will gather, in a different football hemisphere here in North Wales, yet through the magic of the FA Cup this Second Division club have found themselves paired with Manchester United, holders of the trophy and the champions. This is Wrexham's fourth round reward for defeating Ipswich Town, one of the Premiership's endangered sides. United, at Old Trafford, now that is something else. Short of Wembley itself, Wrexham and their fans could not ask for more.

To see this one they do not mind paying full whack and, inevitably, 'life-long supporters' are coming out of the woodwork, desperate for tickets. Gary Bennett is grateful a touch of flu has kept him away from the ground and out of pestering distance for a day or two. But don't worry, he reassures everyone, he'll be fit and ready for United. Do you think he would miss this one?

Bennett converted the decisive penalty against Ipswich. His bare-chested, Italian-style celebration is the enduring image of the third round. He could be forgiven for tearing off his jersey and basking in the glow of his Indian summer. It must have felt like a hair shirt these past eight years. For Bennett, the elation of scoring goals more frequently than any other player in the Football League or Premiership and confronting United are matched only by the sense of relief that he has finally been purged for the serious injury inflicted on a fellow professional.

Bennett was born in Liverpool and fits the popular caricature of a Scouser. He is a tenacious competitor – or a 'scrapper' as they would say on Merseyside – and tends to have plenty to say for himself. He brings a buzz to a team and a dressing-room. A whole army of such players, unable to forge a career with Liverpool or Everton, have roamed the surrounding area, seeking work with smaller teams.

Many resign themselves to non-League and amateur football until a scout backs a hunch and an unlikely opportunity presents itself. Bennett made an impact in the local game and was invited to play for Wigan Athletic. In 1985 he joined Chester for the first time and it was in his second season with the club that he made the trip across the Pennines for that fateful fourth round encounter with Sheffield Wednesday. He clashed with Ian Knight, an England Under-21 defender, who suffered a double compound fracture of the leg.

Knight eventually resumed playing but drifted into the lower divisions. Bennett's place in near obscurity, it seemed, was confirmed. His notoriety preceded him. A new 'Psycho' was in our midst, according to some of his fans, but it was a nickname he could have done without.

'My career took a backward step after that happened,' Bennett says. 'It affected me, no doubt about that. And it affected the attitude of other people and players in the game towards me. They made up their own minds about what happened that day at Hillsborough, but there's no way I did it intentionally. There's no way I would deliberately try to break an opponent's leg or injure him at all. It's a hard game. You have to compete. We all know that. I was just competing. If I'd been the one hurt nothing would have been said. I was nobody. But because Ian Knight was an Under-21 international and they showed it on TV there was a lot of fuss.

'I was labelled the bad boy and that was it as far as most people were concerned. They didn't want to know. I got involved in one or two incidents with other players. Things were said to me by opposition players on the pitch. There was a lot of provocation.

It was hard to hold back and stay out of trouble. My game suffered. It was bound to.'

Bennett had a spell with Southend before returning to Chester and, although his final contribution of the 1991–92 season helped the club avoid relegation from the old Third Division, he could not agree terms for a new contract. 'We went to Stoke needing a win and I scored the only goal of the game,' Bennett says. 'But I couldn't accept what they offered me at the end of the season. They offered me a £5 a week rise and only a one-year deal. I wanted a two-year contract to have a bit of stability and security. But it wasn't only that. At Chester I'd mostly been playing on the wing and I preferred to play down the middle. In the end I said "bye-bye" and really Harry McNally, who was the manager, did me a big favour. Things started to look up for me after that.

'I played for Darlington in a friendly, against Ipswich, and scored. But Wrexham came in and I liked what Brian Flynn had to say. He asked me where I preferred to play and said I could play down the middle for him. I knew the kind of football he and Wrexham liked to play – positive, attractive football – so it was Wrexham for me.'

Flynn, a tiny, gentle man, would not seem the obvious manager to get the best out of Bennett, but he has done so. The goals have flowed. Bennett repaid Flynn with 23 in his first season, 39 in his second. Curious scouts from bigger clubs, still concerned about his old reputation, have been taking a look. If they remain unconvinced, Bennett has noticed a significant change in the attitude of opposing players towards him.

'Players have actually come up to me and said I'm not what people say I am. After all I'd had to put up with it was nice to know people saw something else in me. I felt people were beginning to respect me for my football and my goals. Let's face it, goals get you more respect in this game than anything else and fortunately they're still going in for me.

'I thought after last season it would be a hard task to follow that and I didn't really know what to expect this season, but here I am, in mid-January, with 32 goals in all competitions. I can't explain it. If I could I'd bottle it and sell it.'

His team-mates will tell you he bottles it and saves it for the matches. He is apparently not the world's greatest trainer. But as long as he delivers when it matters, they and Flynn are not going to complain. Nor are the fans. He is a star here. Even his mother has assumed celebrity status. They say she has been asked for her autograph at her local supermarket.

Surely, though, it must be galling for Bennett that all this has come to him at the age of 31. In the era of the £7 million striker, he must ponder what might have been?

'It's no good looking back,' he says. 'What has happened in my career has happened. There's no point in thinking, "This might have happened, or that might have happened." I'm enjoying my football here at Wrexham, playing the style of football they and Brian Flynn believe in. This is a tremendous club, such a friendly club. I'm thankful to be a part of it. But it's also an ambitious club. We're really desperate to get to the First Division. We want to keep progressing and win things. I can get my satisfaction out of that. I can appreciate what I've got here and what I've hopefully still got to come.

'You've got to look forward, to the future. That's what matters and that's what I'm interested in. And look what we've got to look forward to – Manchester United at Old Trafford. You can't get much better than that, can you?

'I can't promise I'll be giving even more because I like to think I give everything, whether it's Connah's Quay Nomads – that was in the Welsh Cup, by the way – or Manchester United. But it's the big one, and you've got to milk it, haven't you? I've been to a few big club-grounds – Tottenham, Arsenal, Forest and Coventry. But never to Old Trafford. It's a great draw for the players and the fans. There'll be a full house, great atmosphere. This is what it's about.

'United are the double winners. If we win, it will be the biggest Cup shock ever. That may be beyond our wildest dreams. You look at it and you say we haven't got a cat in hell's chance, but there's one thing going for us – the FA Cup. And strange things happen in the FA Cup. There's no way we'll go for a draw. We'll attack, as we always do, and we'll score. I'm sure of it. What concerns me is how many we'll let in.'

And if Bennett scores, will there be more shirt-stripping jubilation?

'We're planning something new. The Ipswich thing came about after all the talk about Aylesbury and their duck-walk. I suggested taking my shirt off, as I'd seen them do in Italian football. But we've got a new one for Old Trafford. You'll have to wait till Saturday to see what it is.'

Bennett did not score at Old Trafford but Kieron Durkan gave Wrexham the lead and the prepared routine was put into motion. Durkan stood in a corner of the pitch as his team-mates fell to their knees before him and paid homage. United picked themselves up off their knees to win 5–2. Wrexham had had their dream.

Klinsmann and Spurs safely negotiated the Altrincham hurdle and, come the penultimate stage, they were still there. Now the talk was of the 'Dream Final', Manchester United versus Tottenham. Everton gave Jürgen and Co a rude awakening, however, defeating them 4–1 at Elland Road. Klinsmann was voted Footballer of the Year by the Football Writers' Association but dismayed Spurs' fans by signing for Bayern Munich. Bennett also moved nearer home to Tranmere.

CHAPTER 11

The Gentle Rover

Tim Flowers, of Blackburn Rovers and England

Blackburn Rovers' new training ground – yes, that is new, too – is not the sort of place you are likely to stumble across by accident. With accurate instructions you may eventually find it somewhere north of Blackburn, towards Clitheroe, left into a pretty, tiny village, through a check-point and what looks like a military base but is apparently now home to a collection of business units, and down into a green bowl. This is Brockhall Training Complex.

If it is unsurprising to discover Jack Walker has bought the players he bought a super-duper training complex, it is equally unamazing to discover it in such an obscure location. Typical Kenny Dalglish, you can hear yourself thinking. Keeps himself to himself and his players to himself. Brings them out to play, gets a result, and returns them to their bunker in the back of beyond. That's Kenny's style, and if it irritates anyone, you sense, he will love it all the more.

This is the general portrayal of the club and manager on the verge of delivering the biggest dividend so far for Walker's investment, the Championship. Dalglish, the man who walked out on Liverpool because he could no longer endure the pressures and expectations there, was lured to this modest club by the challenge and seemingly limitless resources offered by Walker, in October 1991. While Dalglish was leading the team from the old Second Division to the top of the Premiership, Walker was ensuring they had a home fit for heroes. New team, new Ewood Park, new training ground. And a new force in English football.

No sooner does a club achieve that status than they attract new detractors. It is the way of the world. But there was a deeper resentment here: a resentment that a top team could be bought overnight; that they quarried rather than sculptured results; that they did it under the management of the perverse and obstructive Kenny Dalglish. The image, like the club, was established.

The image down in the green bowl is of an oasis. A newly built oasis: a low building surrounded by tarmac. The players' cars are parked neatly. Only a couple of service vans spoil the perfect symmetry. But for the cars, you might take this for a small primary school. Once you are through the glass door, opened with great comic performance by Chris Sutton, you feel it could be youth club night. In one corner they are playing pool; in another table tennis. Some are sitting at refectory-type tables, eating lunch; others, including younger, as yet unknown players, are sitting chatting, putting their game if not the world to rights.

Sutton takes a seat near Alan Shearer and the two strikers wade into their mail. Sutton jokes at his own expense, anticipating what he is about to read: 'Has ability, lacks personality ...' He raises more laughs when he flukes a pot on the pool table, but this time it is at the expense of a disbelieving opponent, Henning Berg. Shearer joins the fun by sabotaging Sutton's game with some rearguard activity. More communal jollity.

Shearer is very much the senior partner. He oozes authority and self-assurance, just as he does on the pitch. Sutton is surprisingly boorish, yet it is easy to forget that although he cost a £5 million transfer fee he is still nowt but a lad. There seems to be a genuine rapport between the two strikers, though Sutton knows his place. Also at the table now is Tim Sherwood, the captain. He has an easy manner, joins in the fun while retaining an air of distinction. The air of a captain.

Strands of banter stretch to a table close to the serving counter. There sit Dalglish, his number two, Ray Harford, and other members of the coaching staff. Dalglish, you imagined, would have his own bunker within the bunker but no, here he is, grinning ear to ear, a part of rather than apart from his squad. A mother hen and her chicks. Maybe here, you begin to suspect, is the key to the vertical rise of Blackburn Rovers.

Of course Dalglish has spent lavishly. He outbid Manchester United and all-comers to sign Shearer for £3.3 million and has bought virtually a whole team, even replacing some of his own, 'phase one' acquisitions. Yet apart from signing obviously good players, Dalglish has signed not so obviously good players and, in just about every case, made them better players. Even Shearer has surpassed most expectations of him. He is now acknowledged as the best striker in England and is pushing back the boundaries of his supremacy with every devastating performance. Dalglish saw something in his character, as well as his ability, that would elevate him above the rest, defying serious injury in the process.

Sherwood, once regarded as an ordinary midfield player, has matured and developed the range of his influence under Dalglish's stewardship; Colin Hendry, retrieved from Manchester City, where he was derided as erratic and irresponsible, has been honed into an outstanding central defender and crucial contributor to the club's cause; Graeme Le Saux has been groomed into an England international and forms, with Berg, perhaps the best full-back pairing in the land; and players like Jason Wilcox and Mark Atkins have been coaxed to new, unsuspected levels of performance.

But then here is a team, a team on the Premiership pitch and a team in this training ground building. At most clubs the players are in their cars and away once training is over. Here they lunch together, play pool and table tennis together and chat together into the afternoon. And all under the doting eyes of Dalglish, a Dalglish bearing no resemblance to his unloved caricature.

A player conspicuous by his absence is Tim Flowers, the goalkeeper. At last he appears through the door from the dressing-room area. He casts an eye over proceedings on the pool table, offers a suitable critique, and quickly sees off his lunch. He is being polite. We have an appointment and he suggests we find a dressing-room, away from the inevitable leg-pulling by his team-mates.

Flowers, who followed Shearer from Southampton, is now ranked one of England's two leading goalkeepers – the other being Arsenal's David Seaman – and an important figure in the Blackburn scheme of things. The scheme of keeping players together, of creating this one-ness, has, Flowers contends, helped Blackburn sustain their progress and their resistance to growing pressures.

'The camaraderie you can see for yourself,' he says. 'The set-up here has helped us get that. Basically what we used to do was train on a public park, which would have been used on the Saturday and Sunday by local teams, and come November the pitches were like a beach, just sand. If you put the ball down it would blow down the pitch, that sort of place. Then, covered in mud, we would have to drive in our cars back to Ewood, have a bath and then everybody would go their separate ways.

'But here, now, after training, you come to the clubhouse and you stay together. You've got the gym, the baths and we're getting a sauna and jacuzzi in there. We've got the restaurant, so you have a bite to eat, a game of pool and you talk. That's how you get a team spirit. You can, at certain stages of a season, get away somewhere for a break from the usual routine, and that can get the spirit back. It worked for us at Southampton. But we build the spirit here, day after day.

'The manager is in there, all of them. The gaffer is class. He takes pressure off the players. He's brilliant at it. If you've had a stinker, you won't catch him telling Fleet Street so. For me, that's a quality manager. The last thing you want is somebody chucking everything at your feet. You feel bad enough as it is. Not that he's had too many chances to do that because the lads have been magnificent. But when we do have an off-day, he'll never criticise us openly. Maybe we'll talk about it in here, but no-one else will know, and that's how a football club should be run. He has our respect for that and we repay him by giving him every single thing we've got.'

I suggest to Flowers that those who think this is no place for alternative comedy ought to think again. 'The public image is very different from the Kenny Dalglish we see,' he concurs. 'He is actually very, very funny. He's very dry.'

Blackburn's sense of humour is repeatedly examined by not only the label of 'the team that Jack bought' but also by the 'boring' mantle they appear to have inherited from Arsenal.

Flowers' response is as dismissive as his laugh. 'The lads are not bothered by all that. All the top clubs are spending major amounts of money on players. And I honestly can't see what right-minded football fan would consider us boring. You very rarely find the top scorers in the League are boring.'

Blackburn have been prepared to sweat out the results when necessary, just as Flowers has been willing to toil to improve every aspect of his game. He considers the training regime that has taken him to the top remains his best insurance to stay there. Hence the last line of Blackburn's defence is usually the last in line for lunch.

'I can only try to impress by all I do at Blackburn and when I get the chance to play for the full England side. That's why I go out there and work two or three hours a day, just to try to be at my best and stay at my best.' Flowers adheres to a routine and work ethic imbued over years of watching and learning from mentors John Burridge, Mike Kelly and Peter Shilton. They taught him the painful meaning of words such as technique, professionalism and dedication. His natural instincts have been tuned, his positional sense enhanced and his appetite for success sharpened.

'John Burridge has been a major influence on my career,' Flowers says. 'I was an apprentice at Wolves when he was there and I came across him again when I moved to Southampton. Just watching him, he gave me the will to train, every single day, to want to work at being a goalkeeper, the way he has done. That will has kept him in the game well into his forties. I'd like to be able to look into the mirror when I'm 40, and hopefully still playing, and say, "Tim, you've done everything you possibly could to be as good as you possibly could." If I can do that I'll be happy. If I ever thought I'd not trained hard enough, or could have done something in my time as a player that would have made me a better goalie and I hadn't done it, then I would resent myself for it. Burridge taught me that. He's a phenomenal trainer, the best trainer I've ever come across.

'Mick Kelly probably got me to Blackburn and into the England set-up. He was a goalie coach for Southampton, Leeds, Sheffield United, a few clubs. We were lucky to get him once, sometimes twice a week and he brought me on, oh . . . 60 per cent. He made me into a better than average goalie, I think. He worked me tremendously on technique. Brilliant.

'I was on holiday, in Crete, when Southampton came in for me. My dad phoned me and said Southampton had bid 70 grand and Wolves had accepted it. Straight away I thought, "Peter Shilton, bloody hell. I'm going to be training with Peter Shilton." I'd been on loan there and went back after a week. I didn't know what had hit me. It was so hard, that, because I didn't really get any special goalkeeping training at Wolves. I went down there and Shilton had all the goalkeepers every single day, working them, and I'd never seen anything like it. That really opened my eyes.

'I had a couple of years in the reserves, one or two games with the first team [*and a couple of spells on loan to Swindon*]. I got my home debut and had my face smashed to bits. Cheek-bone went, jaw and everything. I was out for a long time. But then I was in the first team for four or five years, really grafting hard and learning from mistakes. But that's where I was lucky enough to have Mick Kelly.

'No disrespect to Wolves and Southampton, but when I was there we probably lost more games than we won, and that teaches you something as well. You take things out of that. It's tough being near the bottom, as we were at Southampton, with everyone saying we were rubbish, we were down, and having that thrown at you all the time. Then, to come out of that, fighting, and to save the club and keep them up, you get a lot out of that. You also appreciate it when you then come to Blackburn and lose very few matches. At home, especially, we have a phenomenal record. We lost to Manchester United here, but that was when we were reduced to ten men.

'I came here in November 1993 and settled in with no problem at all. In fact I felt I'd settled in within a week of being here. I was lucky in that Alan Shearer was here but then when you've played first team football for a little while you meet these players anyway, playing against them or at different functions.'

You get the impression it would be difficult not to get on with Flowers. Goalkeepers are traditionally a race apart, madcap loners if not a hair-brained dive from the funny farm. Burridge, for instance, is one of the game's great characters, an identikit eccentric. Some modern goalkeepers have become snarling 'Mr Angry' clones, but Flowers tends to be as patient and composed on the field as he is off it. The not-so-wild Rover values his temperament. Coincidentally – or perhaps not – his main rival for the national job is another of nature's cool dudes.

'I think that's just the way I've been since I was born,' says 28-year-old Flowers, who hails from Kenilworth. 'I think I was always easy to talk to and get along with. I've always had time for most people. And I think on the pitch, even if you're a bit nervous, it helps the team if you don't show it.

'I tell you who's a master at it, Dave Seaman. He always gives that unflappable air, even if he's made a mistake. He'll just put out that calming hand of his and say, "No problem, no problem." And that's the best way. It's what your team-mates want to see. They want someone who's steady, law of averages type, the type you know where he's going to be at most given times. Defenders don't like to see goalkeepers haring past them. If the ball's knocked over the top they like to know you're backing them up. If it's a big match, great atmosphere, everything, it just gives them that bit of coolness they want from a goalkeeper. I'll still get plenty of ribbing for any little mishap, as all keepers do, but we learn to live with that.

'I think basically the thing with me is that I enjoy playing football and would want to continue playing football whatever. If professional football went out of the window tomorrow, I would play it for nothing. People read about the fees and the wages and maybe find that hard to believe, but it's the truth. I've played football since I was old enough to walk. I love winning, but above all else I love playing.

'I enjoy football. I enjoy training almost as much as the games. I enjoy just coming in every day, seeing the lads, having that dressing-room banter. When you talk to people like Terry Gennoe, who coaches us now, or any ex-pro, they all tell you they miss their playing days. They miss that day-to-day camaraderie. If you ask them for their advice, they always say to you, "Don't hang up your boots too early, play as long as you can.' Going back to John Burridge, look at him.

'Of course there are going to be times when you think you are hard done by and I admit I sometimes have a go at referees, but I never really mean it. If there's a corner and someone is standing on me I might say, "Hey ref, watch him", just in case I get a foul out of him. I don't think you see too many goalkeepers chase refs and linesmen. They don't really get the chance, do they? They're in that box and that's them.'

Goalscorers have traditionally tended to enjoy greater glory and wealth than goalsavers, and Flowers welcomes the opportunity to communicate a grievance of his trade. 'I'll do my bit for the union and say I think 'keepers are still somewhat underrated compared with strikers. I think it's of paramount importance to have a good goalkeeper in your team. If you haven't, you're not going to do anything . . . '

Flowers' argument is interrupted by ostentatious snores from outside the dressing-room door.

'Goalkeepers are worth as much as forwards, without a doubt,' he continues, turning up the volume for the benefit of his ear-wigging team-mate. 'Forwards are uglier, as well.'

The message presumably received by one A Shearer, Flowers reduces the decibels again and continues: 'It's been traditional that goalkeepers have gone for a song and you've always paid your money for forwards. I don't think that really bothers goalkeepers. They know their job's every bit as important, and what matters to them is doing it to the best of their ability.'

Flowers recognises – quietly, of course – that Shearer is a special case. 'Alan has found a new dimension here. He's the most recognisable footballer in Britain and rightly so. He's a class act. I think you could compare him to Mark Hughes in his body make-up, in the way he plays. He's very strong, immensely powerful shot, good in the air. I don't think anyone would dispute he's the best forward around. But we're very lucky in England at the moment. Our game is absolutely littered with top quality strikers.'

Another quality player is Matthew Le Tissier, voted second behind Shearer in the PFA's Player of the Year Awards. Shouldn't he also follow Shearer's lead by taking his talent from Southampton to a more progressive club? You won't catch Flowers off his line with that one.

'That's up to Matt,' he fends with a smile. 'But I can say this from personal experience. He put probably the goal of the season past me and some of the other goals he's scored this season have been quite magnificent, so judging by that I would say he doesn't have to move to produce his best. Matt knows what he wants to do. He's no mug.'

Flowers knows what he wants and it would seem he's no mug, either.

'When I came here I said I really thought Blackburn would win something and now I'm convinced, whether it's sooner or later, they will. They are a young team, so they've got them for years to come. Presumably they also have money to spend if they require it. If the right player comes along, they will be in there, to improve the team. That says to me that they will continue to go forward and win things.

'Nobody here has ever shouted about our League position because we know what can happen in this game. Even when we've been red hot and put ourselves in a strong position for the Championship we've not got carried away. Man United have had the advantage of knowing what it takes to win the title. That can make a big difference.

'I've always wanted to win a gong of some sort, something to have at the end of my career. Something I can remember. Having been a winner, actually having won something. You know what I mean? And I'd love to add to my collection of caps. Terry Venables has made it very plain that he will be keeping an eye on both David Seaman and me. Obviously, he's trying to sort out his jigsaw.'

Flowers finds respite from the business of chasing honours enjoying the simple life at his home in Birkdale, Southport.

'I like gardening, when the weather's good enough, and I like just playing with the kids. I've got two little girls. They take up a lot of time. That's about it, really, outside football. I don't do a lot else, to be honest. I like to get home and rest. You can get very tired, very quickly in our season. There are pressures playing a lot of big, important games, but they are the right pressures. You want to be playing at the top level for as long as you can, and that's why you try to maintain your fitness . . . '

The snoring prowler is back at the door, reaching inside, asking for the car keys. Flowers rolls his eyes. Perhaps it's time to go home and rest, anyway.

Blackburn, despite defeat at Liverpool on the last day of the season, won their first championship since 1914. Mission accomplished, Dalglish moved upstairs to become director of football, leaving Harford to take over as team manager.

CHAPTER 12

Facts of International Life

Terry Venables, England coach

The most thankless task in football? It has to be a toss up between refereeing and managing the national team. The men in black, green, red, yellow and grey accept criticism, even abuse, as an occupational hazard. But then one match pretty quickly merges into the next and it's someone else's turn to take the flak. When you are in charge of the team that represents the country, the stakes are higher and although success can earn acclaim, even a knighthood, anything less brings condemnation of a brutal, abhorrent nature.

How things have changed since the days of the gentleman commander, Walter Winterbottom. The job, like the game, is now constantly high profile, subject to the whims of the tabloid Press and the nerves at Lancaster Gate. Sir Alf Ramsey, having won the World Cup for England in 1966, was unfortunate to confront the magnificent Brazilians in 1970 but ran out of support and sympathy when he dug in his heels too far and failed the next time round.

The avuncular Joe Mercer kept the seat warm for a succession of perceived under-achievers or nearly men. Don Revie became increasingly uncomfortable and escaped to the desert; many saw Ron Greenwood as too smug and clever by half; depending on your point of view, Bobby Robson was either lucky or unlucky at Italia '90; and Graham Taylor, dubbed 'Turnip' by one national newspaper, plunged himself deeper into the mire with his touchline video nasty. Respect, it seemed, was no longer an essential companion for the ultimate badge of office.

And then came Terry Venables. Now here was a man who knew a thing or two about flak. His fall-out with Irving Scholar soured his first alliance at White Hart Lane, and a still more bitter and costly bust-up with Alan Sugar ended his Tottenham dream. Legal proceedings over Venables' claim for wrongful dismissal, plus allegations regarding financial dealings – all denied and none proven – must have made him pine for the mere hysteria of Barcelona.

*Well, when you've done just about everything there is to be done in football –
Venables alone has played for England at every level, a niche in history assured
forever because the amateur team no longer exists; he won the Spanish League
and the League Cup at Camp Nou; and the FA Cup as player and manager of
Spurs – and made your mark outside as an author and script-writer, the opportunity to take charge of the national side has to figure as the last great challenge.*

*The FA, having deployed Jimmy Armfield to scour the land for candidates
and opinions on candidates, eventually came to the conclusion that Venables
should be their man and the appointment of the new England coach, rather than
manager, was announced on Friday 28 January 1994. The accompanying wall-
to-wall media coverage conveyed the consensus of approval and, more than a year
into his tenure, his England team remained unbeaten.*

*Already, however, you sensed the honeymoon with some sections of the Press
was over. England were uninspiring against Uruguay and were losing until
hooligans forced the abandonment of the match in Dublin. These were friendly
encounters, of course, because, as hosts of the 1996 European Championship,
England automatically qualified. Venables was keen to explore the possibilities,
both in terms of personnel and tactics. But the rumblings of discontent were coming through loud and clear.*

So this is the England job. On reflection, perhaps refereeing is a doddle, after all.

When he's not with the England team, at his Lancaster Gate
office, watching a game, at a meeting, or in a television studio, the chances are you'll catch Venables at his Kensington dining
club, Scribes West. His second wife, Yvette ('Toots' to her friends),
keeps the place running smoothly and allows the England boss the
luxury of an occasional quiet meal. Scribes is very Kensington: pas-
tel shades, Chesterfields and tinkling ivories. The whiff of cigar
smoke leads the trail to Tel's table, in the far corner.

Start talking football, and he is still, at the age of 52, the East
End kid who learned and honed his skills in the street; the cheeky
lad who always had plenty to say for himself; the devoted son who
never forgot his roots. The manager in the making was apparently
as obvious as the potential player.

'I was always a sort of organiser, a busy sod, really,' he recalls.
'My mum felt when I was about 15 that I actually wanted to be a
coach or a manager more than a player. I took my coaching badge at
a fairly young age and I was always interested in coaching and,

without knowing it at the time, preparing myself early on for later days.

'You can contrast that, for example, with the case of George Graham. I signed him from Portsmouth for Crystal Palace. He hadn't actually thought of what he was going to do and he was about 31 then. He became very successful his way and I think I've been reasonably successful my way. It just goes to show there are many ways of going about it.

'I'm not sure whether you are necessarily interested in coaching as such at that stage. What you are really interested in is the game and how to get better at it, how to get better at it as individuals and how we can get percentages out of it by being better in a structural way – within the team and within various systems of play. When we were at Chelsea we were interested in coaching and management and football itself. We felt there were ways of improving our game.

'It was at the time when coaching was beginning to take off but had a bit of a bad name. People started saying it was coaching ability out of the players, which was nonsense. You get good and bad coaches like you get good and bad journalists or whatever else. Big Mal [*Malcolm Allison*] was with the West Ham Academy, as they used to call it, and that really started the coaching thing. We came later, at Chelsea, and it got bigger and bigger.

'I can't recall a point where I ever thought . . . "England." Certainly not early on, anyway. In fact, just when I started to think it might be for me some time, I got the chance to go to Barcelona and I put it right out of my mind. To be honest, it seemed to me that the England job was one you just couldn't win. Yes, you fancy it, but the odds are stacked so heavily against you.

'Then I chose to go to Tottenham, a club I had always loved and of course played for. I had the chance to involve myself in ownership, to commit myself totally and invest my money in it. I wanted to make it successful as a football club and successful financially over a long period of time. That, as everyone knows, wasn't to be. I had a lot of aggravation with Sugar and my ambition got crushed. When the England opportunity came along I think I suited the FA and it suited me at that time. But if it hadn't been for that situation with Sugar I would still have been at Tottenham.

'I would say the job is much as I expected. You know it is going to be difficult on the football side because there are so many top teams across Europe and around the world these days. I just get disappointed with the lack of thought from some sections of the Press. Criticism doesn't bother me at all, but the ludicrous observations some of them make and the articles they write are well out of order.

'The media in this country are getting more and more aggressive. Abroad I found they tried to analyse football more. We have got papers that do that but we've got others that don't and you find you are a victim of all that unnecessary and unjustified stuff they throw at you. I got slagged by a couple of experienced journalists for supposedly getting Premiership fixtures called off for a squad get-together when in fact the weekend was always going to be free for the benefit of the other home countries playing European qualifying ties.

'I could say I'm not going to say more than I have to, but then that is unfair to those decent people who care about the game and want to do an honest job. That's why I prefer to do interviews one on one now. I mean, it's a sad state of affairs when I can't sit down at a Press conference for England and discuss football. Eight- or nine-tenths of that audience are interested in what I have got to say. It makes them think about something and they go away and write about it in a reasonable way, whereas there is this other small element and I know that if I say so-and-so's not playing well at the moment it will be taken right out of context. It's "Venables disregards X forever". I simply can't say what I want to these people. It's just very sad when you can't have a discussion with the Press as a whole.'

Is Matt Le Tissier a case in point?

'All players are a case in point,' he parries with trained reflexes. 'All players. They've made the point that I was trying to build a team round Paul Gascoigne, that I gave him special consideration and all the rest of it, but I never have. I've never built around anyone. It's a stupid comment, just as it would be stupid of me to do that. If you've got a very good player – and I don't think many people dispute Gascoigne is a very good player – he's an asset to your team. He actually comes on top of your team but he doesn't come before the team. The faces may change but the team will always be there. I could spend two years building a team around Paul Gascoigne, then he gets injured and what have I got? Very little.'

The Le Tissier issue is one of those teasers football never seems to be able to solve or agree upon. His talent is unquestioned. He is a conjurer of magical moments, capable of outrageous goals and has, for the past two seasons, almost single-handedly kept Southampton in the Premiership. His manager, Alan Ball, does not mind admitting that he builds his team around Le Tissier and never misses an opportunity to wonder aloud why he is not a fixture in Venables' team.

Since Venables studiously avoids public debate over individual players, let us consider his possible thought process. Now he, as the man in charge of England and the man judged on England's results, would have to be some sort of mug not to pick what he believes to be his best team. There are times when you do not bite your nose to spite your face. So presumably Venables is not convinced the package Le Tissier has to offer – ability, application and contribution to the team effort – will improve his England.

History records that some of the most gifted players were not always trusted at the highest level. The likes of Rodney Marsh, Stan Bowles, Tony Currie and Frank Worthington might have achieved more and many would argue they should have had the chance to achieve more. But not everyone was convinced they deserved greater opportunity. Alf Ramsey knew he was risking the wrath of the nation when he left out the mercurial Jimmy Greaves, but England won the World Cup and the case for the prosecution collapsed.

'I prefer to discuss any weakness a player needs to work on with the player concerned and not in the media,' Venables say. 'It's like someone having the hardest shot in the world. That's all very well, but if he never gets a shot at goal it's of no value. I'm not going on holiday with players. I'm looking for success and if I favour someone it's normally because I think he's a better player. That's the only favour I've given and will continue to give. In the end I've got to come down to 11 players and they will be chosen by what I see in the next 14 months or whatever it is.

'Everybody has an opinion on who should be playing for England, of course. People in the street, cab drivers, fans at different grounds, are all quick to give you advice. When Andy Cole was at Newcastle everyone on Tyneside was telling me I'd got to put Cole in. He goes to Man United and the Geordies don't want him any-more. Now it's Man United supporters who want Cole in. It depends who they support and they can't get away from that.

'But really, when it's an international, whoever's playing for the England side should be supported right through the country. You can't pick a team to make everyone happy. You can't do the job on everyone else's terms. Once you are in the job it's got to be on your terms. You've got to be single-minded. You've got to be the man.

'I know in my mind exactly what I want and I know exactly where I'm going. I'm not going to be so inflexible as to say this is it or that is it. There will always be someone doing something outstanding who will come into the picture and of course you are prepared to accommodate a player in such a situation. But a year or so along the line and I'm quite happy where I am. I would have settled for where I am and in a very short time, coming out of the summer tournament, I'll have, for better or worse, a clearer idea of ourselves and the opposition because we've got two of the best teams in the world in the competition.'

Those two leading national teams being Brazil and Sweden, while ambitious Japan complete the quartet for a tournament intended to add a little more competitive edge to England's preparations.

'We're finding out where we are,' Venables resumes. 'I can't possibly say at this moment where we are. I'm not trying to hedge. We have had a poor record, we're trying to improve and I think we are improving. There is some arrogance in this country, from supporters and Press, even people in the game, that we are among the best. The facts do not support that. It's not where you start, it's where you finish. We haven't won anything at international level since '66, and before that nothing.

'Being at home for the European Championship is not a disadvantage and it may be more of an advantage, I don't know, but again the fact is that no country has won this competition or the World Cup at home for coming up to 12 years.' [*France were crowned European champions in Paris, in 1984.*]

One of the few utterances to spill from Alf Ramsey's lips was the unequivocal, matter-of-fact pledge to the nation that England would win the World Cup in 1966. Will Venables be predicting success in 1996?

An equally emphatic 'No' is his response. 'No, I won't be saying that. Alf maybe saw something, knew something, felt something, I don't know.'

The FA patently believed Venables' knowledge of the Continental game would strengthen England's prospects. The coach is endeavouring to educate his players in the wiles of Europe's élite while retaining the best of the traditional, fundamental English qualities.

'Change of pace is important. If your game is fast all the way through a match you're pressurising your own ability. I'm not saying you can't succeed that way, but it can make things easier for the opposition. Again, the results support that belief. We don't want to try and copy the teams that perhaps do it better than us, either, so it's a case of keeping what we do well, then adding to it. A lot of the Continental opposition don't like playing the English for certain reasons. We must not discard those weapons. I don't think that's a compromise, it's a development.

'The style of football in the Premiership is exciting. Everyone likes it. It's successful. I think it's been successful for television and the viewer. I've enjoyed it as much as when I was at Barcelona watching Spanish football. The beauty of the game is that you can see it and enjoy it in various forms and for different reasons all over the world. Whether your taste is the aggressive, powerful type of game, or the slower, artistic style, it's out there. I love the game in many forms and for different reasons. Sure, there are some bad matches, but then that makes you appreciate the good ones even more.'

English football has celebrated and fêted its goalscorers of late and there is a general perception that Venables is blessed with a surfeit of high calibre strikers. He takes a more cautious view.

'There are more goals here than anywhere else, so that sort of environment has to help front players. It's more of a gung-ho, up-and-down type of game here, isn't it? Whereas in Italy and Spain it's more solid, they don't give you so many chances, it's much harder to score goals. Once more, look at the facts. Strikers haven't scored 30-odd goals when they've gone to Italy. So I don't know where our strikers rate. That is something we have to find out.'

A setback to England's game plan beyond Venables' control was the crowd violence which forced the abandonment of the match against the Republic of Ireland. Anger and contempt were etched in

Venables' countenance that evening at Lansdowne Road. He is, however, as resolved to defy the thugs as he is to resist all those he considers enemies of his game.

'The hooliganism aspect affects me and appals me, though it's not something I can actually do anything about. But then there have been a number of elements around the game which have disappointed me, yet they do not affect the game and they do not dissolve my enthusiasm for the game. It's the people around the game who cause the problems, it's the people in the stadium who fight. My love of the game only gets stronger. Rather than think it's not worth all the aggro and give in, I go the other way. We won't be beaten by these people.

'Some people seem to think it's first time round for problems in football and that the game is finished. Nonsense. There have always been problems but the game is too strong to be affected. At the same time we have to make sure we set the right standards in the game and give the players the guidance they need. I think the English game has adopted a very responsible attitude towards drugs, for instance. I'm very committed to the campaign against drugs. We have to be sure the players have the rules spelled out to them.

'Chris Armstrong may have been surprised he was not allowed to play for a while because he felt there was nothing particularly wrong in what he did. The players have to know exactly where they stand, what the penalty is going to be and if they are thrown out of the game they have no complaints because the excuse has been taken away.

'I thought the Paul Merson situation was handled well by the FA and by the player himself. If he hadn't come out with all that it would have been bubbling beneath the surface and affected him. I've been impressed with him. It's been tough for him and he needs and deserves support. If we lay down rules and they still want to abuse them, then I have no sympathy, but in this situation I do prefer the sympathetic approach and Paul Merson could be a part of my plans in future. Tony Adams came through his ordeal [*the Arsenal captain was jailed for a drink-driving offence*] to play magnificently for his club and his country. People can come back from things like that a lot stronger.'

The strength of a manager's character is constantly examined but Jack Charlton, the English World Cup winner who performed a minor miracle by carrying the Republic of Ireland to the higher echelons of international football, has repeatedly made it known he would walk away if he sensed he no longer had the faith of the people.

'I haven't thought like that because I haven't got that far along the line,' Venables says. 'Jack's been very successful, in a much easier atmosphere. He's done a magnificent job for Ireland. Football hasn't traditionally been their top sport but it has become so tremendously popular there because of Jack. He's reached the stage where he should be able to do whatever he wants and shouldn't be criticised. I'm not at that stage.

'It is difficult to say precisely what would be successful for us in the Championships. It depends how we play. If we lost badly and didn't play well, that would be a failure. If we didn't get as far as I thought we should have but were unfortunate, I might see that in a different light. It would have to be what was in my mind. If I felt I'd failed then that would be my failure, no-one else's. And I'd be my own critic, my own judge.'

Venables' England suffered their first defeat against Brazil, at Wembley, in the deciding match of the Umbro tournament.

CHAPTER 13

Hand of God

Canon JR Smith, vice-chairman of Bury

The centre of Bury is much the same as any town centre now, the remnants of its past trapped by ring roads, diversions and pedestrian streets. Some will even tell you the much and long acclaimed market is not what it was, but then what is? Especially along the industrial ribbon that wrapped around Manchester?

At the far end of The Rocks, however, there is salvation for many a persuasion, a rewind to Olde Englande. The Two Tubs Inn gleams white and inviting, the very vision of a hostelry to cheer the soul and defy time. Opposite stands a very different building; a stone structure, more upright, dignified, but another bastion of the right order of things. This, too, offers spiritual solace. The board confirms this is Bury Parish Church, St Mary the Virgin. It goes on to inform: Baptisms, weddings and funerals with Canon JR Smith by appointment. The Rectory telephone number is also given.

It is more than 20 years since the town's football club called on Canon Smith for assistance, divine or otherwise. They invited him on to their board of directors. He became vice-chairman and ever since has tended his flock at Gigg Lane as well as here, at the Parish Church.

Bury Football Club is not what it was, either. At the turn of the century and again for a spell in the 'Twenties, they played in the First Division (when, of course, the First Division was the first division) and finished the 1925–26 season a lofty fourth. In 1900 and again in 1903 they won the FA Cup. We are talking heritage here.

Alas for Bury, the competition in Lancashire was to take its toll. This was destined to be one of the small clubs, those cosy little corners of our game that would occasionally flicker and catch the attention of a patronising nation with an unlikely Cup run and stir normally indifferent natives, only to return to the reality of their bread-and-butter existence, relying on the emergence of some bright young thing to flog to fat cats of the big cities, or a whip-round among the directors. This is football life light years away from the Premiership.

Bury have, indeed, had to sell to survive and have been grateful for the generosity of benefactors. They have hired out their ground to Manchester United for reserve team fixtures and to Swinton Rugby League club. But now club and team are in the ascendancy. The abuse for the manager, Mike Walsh, has turned to songs of praise for the way he has guided Bury into a Third Division play-off place. The ground, too, is developing nicely, not only as the home for the town's professional footballers but for the town's brethren.

The satisfaction and pleasure begin to radiate when at last you find your way to the wooden Rectory gates, walk up the drive, pass the first of spring's rhododendrons, towards a surprisingly modern house, through a front door opening to the sound of bells and left into a small study. Canon Smith sits at his bureau, seemingly hemmed in by stacks of books and papers, penning his latest discourse. No, it is not a sermon – or at least he hopes it is not – but a speech to be delivered at a cricket dinner that evening.

Football? Cricket? 'Yes, I suppose I was always a sportsman,' he says, swivelling on his chair and revealing, beneath a grey jacket, his dog-collar. 'I played football in Radcliffe [*an even smaller town in these parts*] for ten years, then I went to St Helens, where I played again. I played a lot of cricket, too. Oh, I love cricket. I've been involved in sport all my life and it's lovely to see Bury doing so well now. Really lovely.'

But what is a nice, venerable man like this doing in a game like this? A man of the cloth directly involved in the game of shame somehow doesn't seem right. Yes, you will see church people at most grounds in the land and Old Trafford is something of a cathedral for Irish Catholic priests. But The Rector is vice-chairman!

'Well, to start with I think they knew me as someone who knew something about football,' he says, taking us back those 20-odd years. 'I had been a Bolton fan because I lived in Atherton [*yet another even smaller town in these parts*], on the other side of Bolton. When I came to Bury I was still quite close to Bolton and I could have gone to either, but I decided to throw in my lot with the local team because my children were interested in Bury. So I started going to Bury and after a year or two I was asked if I'd like to be a director.

'There was a bit of a hiatus at the club. There was someone trying to get into the club that they weren't happy about and I was asked to become a member. Sam Lord, who was a director at that time, took me down to Reading with the team one Saturday. I didn't know why, except it was a nice outing but I discovered it was to see if I could possibly fit in with what was going on. So I helped the fellow to wheel the truck with the kit, we changed trains in London and we got to Reading, and we won in the last minute. I suppose they thought that was a good omen and after we came back they asked me to join the club.

'The first away match after was at Barnsley and we won 1–0, which we didn't generally do. When the match was over the chairman of Barnsley called me back and our chairman, Billy Allen, and the others were worried. "What's he said? Has he upset him or something?" they were asking. So they asked me what he wanted. In fact, he wanted to know if I thought the vicar of Barnsley knew anything about football because I'd obviously done them some good.

'So that was where we started and it's gone on from there. Now I've got lots of friends, in the club, in football, and around the town. They perhaps think I do more for football than I do for the church but that's not true. They know I'm football mad, but I still have to keep a level head. It is unusual for a churchman to be a vice-chairman, certainly. There are chaplains all over the country, but I don't know of anyone who's actually a director.

'The chaplains do a good job and we have a part to play in sport. Ray Illingworth didn't think so for the England cricket team, did he? He bounced their chaplain, who was a nephew of the former Rector here, Winfield Digby. Illy changed his mind a little bit afterwards, though. You mustn't do too much of ramming the idea of the church down, but I'm there and they know I'm there. They can get in touch with me if they want me. They can talk to me, I can talk to them. But it's the fact that we are involved and the church is involved and a lot of my people are involved.

'Money didn't enter into it at all. They never asked me for anything. Anything I've given to the club or leant to the club or done for the club was because I wanted to, not because they asked me to. We've all played our part. Our chairman, Terry Robinson, is a working chairman. He's actually the chief executive, if you like.

He doesn't just pop in. He's done a fantastic job and puts in an awful lot of time. He's got us these grants and help along the way.

'Hugh Eaves, a Bury man originally but from London now, put the money in to get us on the road and give us a bit of stability. He's been an excellent man. He comes up for almost every match. And Fred Mason and John Smith – the other director called Smith; we get muddled up at times but I'm JR, or Reg, as they call me – do marvellously for the club. We are just a group of men who love the place and love the club.'

It is just as you imagine a small town club, run by a board of self-made men, chummy and snug. And by now people in the town and the club, and in towns and clubs up and down the country, have become accustomed to the man of God with the eloquence, sharp wit and ready smile.

'People don't react badly at all to me,' he says, 'Things people tend to say to me are good-humoured. Some teams will say, "What chance have we today with you on their side?" I don't think the players are uneasy with me. There's no sense of stand-offishness. We get on well together. Sometimes I get called Rector but then that's my title. It's what I get paid for. In the football club I get respect and I don't need anything else. It can be a bit embarrassing when something's gone wrong and they come to me or write me a letter saying they're surprised I've allowed the club to do this or that, but you can't stop everything, can you? But I've never really had any trouble.

'Directors at other clubs are always very friendly. I've been seeing some of them for 20-odd years. I miss some away matches because of weddings and things. I've had a good year from that angle. The weddings are going hell for leather now. I love weddings. I love my people and I don't get upset if I can't go to football. There are plenty of matches over a season and you can get your money's worth if you're faithful.

'I don't tell people when to get married. I point out the fact that if they want late weddings in November and that sort of thing, they'll get no photographs worth seeing because they'll be coming out in the dark. They haven't thought of that, you see. Photographs are very important to every wedding.

'I don't think people come to church because of my connections with Bury. I'm sure they don't. I hope they come to church for what they get. That's my job and the thing I love as well. I don't have any problems reconciling the church with football. If I can go to football I'm happy to go. I think football is a wonderful game, played as it should be, a contest between two teams who come out at the end of it friendly.

'It's something that doesn't take all day or night. You can do a morning's work and your evening's work, and when you've worked every other day of the week you can afford to have a few hours off. I'm always here. I call myself available – where they want you, where they need you. If the phone goes my wife or I will get it. We're on the ball.

'On a Sunday morning I generally get comments like "Aren't we doing well?" or the next week "What were you doing yesterday?" When we lose I'm to blame, when we win they enjoy the success. It's good to be able to enjoy it now because we went through hard times and literally had to put our bank book in the hands of the bank manager to carry on. Now we've got a lovely ground and plans to do all sorts of things.

'We've got three sides covered with seating accommodation and we're going to cover the other one. We've got a grant to lay down things for the community. We've got pitches for women to play netball or whatever it is they want to play and we've got accommodation for community service. We are football in the community, as it is called, and there's a lovely, sort of family spirit. We've had one or two grants for what we've done for the blind. We've provided special seats for the blind and someone tells them what's happening in the match. There are lots of things that really make it worthwhile.

'And at the moment we know we are in the play-offs. We'd like to be in the top two for automatic promotion, but they can't knock us out of the play-offs this year. The team are very strong at the moment and have come from nowhere. We had a rough spell and didn't do well for a few weeks. Our centre-forward was injured, so were one or two others and people were banned and one thing and another. Then we suddenly came good.'

But not all in and around the game is good, as Canon Smith glumly concedes. 'The bad language and the foul-mouthed chanting doesn't please me. It doesn't please any decent man. You can't take children to matches if you've got that sort of thing going on and we would like to clean up football. You have the idiots but you can't legislate for idiots, can you? That's one of my favourite expressions. And if they decide to be idiots then they're idiots. Some of the language sometimes ... well. When we were having a bad spell, of course, it was "Walsh out" and "We've paid for rubbish" and all this.

'But you go and watch a schoolboy football match and listen to the dads on the line. They're worse than we are. They get so wrapped up in it and they forget that the kids are 11 and 12 or, at the oldest, 15 and 16. The language is terrible in some of those matches. I never swore when I was playing in amateur football, for my Sunday school team, or at university or whatever, the referees were pretty firm, told the players to shut up and they did.'

'Anyway, now we're having a good run and nothing's said. People are happy. We have only about two and a half thousand people you can call really regular supporters. We get the others on special days, you know, against Rochdale, or when Carlisle, the top club, came, that sort of thing. We had a good turnout at Wigan and we've got faithful people who follow us all over the country. If you love Bury you follow the club. I still love Bolton, as well. Nat Lofthouse comes to see us when Bolton are away. We get on well together, no trouble at all.

'The money at the top of the game doesn't please me. I think the Premier League will soak the others out if we don't watch what we are doing. The same thing is starting to happen in Rugby League, because of what television are offering them. Television runs football in a sense. They tell you you'll play at five o'clock or four o'clock and what day you'll play, and I think it's time the football people said, "We'll play at three o'clock on Saturday afternoon and be damned to your money."

'The clubs wouldn't like that, but when you read that the top clubs get so many thousands for being on telly and they don't take the little clubs ... Only the Premier League is wanted but there should be a place for everybody. I mean, where do all the footballers come from? Bolton played at Wembley [*against Liverpool, in the Coca Cola Cup final*] the other week, bless 'em, and it was great. There were three ex-Bury players playing. They're all over the country. The Keegans and all the others have come from lowly clubs and got their way to the top and I say, "Well done." But don't forget where

121

they learned it all. Don't forget the schoolmaster who first taught them how to kick a ball, how to play in a team.

'So we have to watch that the Premier clubs don't choke us out of existence and we are in a very bad spot. We've got Bolton, Burnley, Blackburn, Preston, Rochdale, United, City – and we're in the middle of that lot. The East Anglian clubs, Norwich and Ipswich, they've nobody near them. It's difficult but if we can keep a decent number of people following us and loyal as they are at the moment, we'll win in the end.'

Are we, though, in danger of losing the fight against sleaze? 'I've no experience of corruption and bribery. Well, I have. I've experienced one act of bribery and corruption but it was before I was a director. Somebody wanted to swing a game but couldn't get the others to go along with it. I don't come across any bribery or corruption now. Certainly we've never been involved in any matches that were thrown. I half hoped Carlisle might not be trying 100 per cent before going to Wembley for their Auto Windscreens final, but they were.

'A lot of things have happened that don't really bring joy to people who love football, and the great thing is that football is for everyone. It's sad when a team says they are going to close down because they can't afford to go on. If you asked a class full of children to name six places in England I guarantee they'll give you six towns with a football team. It matters that much.

'I'm speaking at the cricket club dinner tonight and I'm just reading about one of their former players who was captain of Lancashire. Brilliant man and nearly 100 years ago. You've got a heritage and a tradition there. Bury have a proud history. Always been about and won the Cup in 1900 and 1903. Bury won 6–0 in 1903, the biggest win in a Cup final and 90-odd years ago. Not bad.'

There is, however, a tinge of sorrow to this nostalgia. The ball used in the 1903 final, so withered it was affectionately known as 'The Prune', went on show in the capital and never returned to Gigg Lane.

'The people running the exhibition went broke, everything was taken and they kept our ball. Bury were a great team in those days. We had a lovely picture of them in the *Bury Times* this week. They say we used to get 20-odd thousand at the games. It's a long time since we had 20-odd thousand but they still remember the great days at Bury. And they were in the First Division for a long time, too, and had their moments.'

Now the 'Shakers' are in the shadows of the great Lancastrian teams. But then Blackburn, not far up the road, have bought their way to their new, towering status.

'You can't all suddenly find people with money who really know the game and throw themselves in. I admire what Jack Walker's done for Blackburn. He's got money so he's used it. If you want to see your team do well and you're willing to pay for the best players, why not? It's not immoral. He can go out and buy an aeroplane, cars, whatever, but he backs his club.

'But let's not forget our roots. If you look back to the beginnings of football there were Sunday school teams and amateur teams from which the other teams have sprung. City were produced by a Sunday school, Barnsley were. You'll see pictures of them in the boardrooms. It came the hard way. I paid tuppence a week in 1920-odd to play football and a penny of that was for insurance. You paid a shilling a week in the 1930s, which was nearly all your spending money. And you went on your bike.

'You wonder about the edge in the Premier League. You wonder about who's going to Wembley for United when they have all those players. You can't have all that great squad playing. That sort of thing worries me a little bit, when a lad plays all season and doesn't get to Wembley.'

There is a local concern here. 'When they played Crystal Palace in the semi-final they had one of our young lads from Bury at right-back, young Gary Neville, and I reckoned he played as well as anybody. I would have given him man of the match.'

Neville's father, Neville – yes, Neville Neville – is Bury's commercial manager and his mother, Jill, is secretary. The couple have a younger son, Philip, who is also with United.

Bury are proud of their 'young lads'. 'Gordon Taylor played for us. He was a great lad and he's been very sensible and very good in his job. We have connections from Bury with all kinds of walks of life and it really matters.'

The after-life also matters to this football man, of course, but will he find his beloved game in heaven?

'Well, there'll be no Sunday football in heaven, tell 'em. I don't know. I think there's peace in heaven, that's the great thing. You get the reward for your work, don't you? And if you get into heaven you'll be surprised at the people who are there and surprised at the people who are not there, I always say, so don't get too upset. I suppose there might be a lot of football people up there.'

Alas, you won't be finding Bury up there in the Second Division. They lost in the play-off final against Chesterfield. Five matches into the 1995/96 season, Bury and Mike Walsh parted company.

CHAPTER 14

The Sorcerer and his Apprentice

Ron Atkinson and Gordon Strachan, manager and player-coach of Coventry City

Unremarkably, Ron Atkinson's phone was constantly engaged that autumn day in 1986. Persistence was eventually rewarded but the mumbled words of commiseration were cut short: 'Get yourself over here,' he said. 'Let's have a party.'

The revelry that proceeded deep into the night at his home in Rochdale has now passed into football folklore. Who else but Big Ron would have responded to his sacking by Manchester United, the biggest club in the land, with a major bash? There again, how else would you have expected Big Ron to react? Pizzas were ordered and one of his players, Gordon Strachan, assumed responsibility for the music. Big Spender and Goldfinger boomed from the stereo. Big Ron loved that, of course. We heard subsequently that the Strachans had taken the wrong turn on to the motorway and instead of arriving home in South Manchester found themselves on the outskirts of Leeds, at Elland Road.

How the strands of football separate and entwine. Strachan, previously of Aberdeen, parted company with Atkinson's successor, Alex Ferguson, previously manager of Aberdeen, a couple of seasons later and joined Leeds United, where he won the League Championship at United's expense. Atkinson, who had twice led United to FA Cup success, had a brief, eventful spell in charge of Atletico Madrid, won the League Cup with Sheffield Wednesday (against United) and with Aston Villa (against United). Dismissed by Villa only a few months after that Wembley triumph, he was to be appointed manager of Coventry City, there to recruit his intended successor, one G Strachan.

This hitherto sedate Premiership cul-de-sac was transformed into a media thoroughfare and hive of activity. Three wins and three draws from the new boss's first six matches eased fears of relegation but then Coventry were bound to stay up, weren't they? Well, they always did. This time, though, the place was alive, even if Alan Shearer's late equaliser for Blackburn at Highfield Road dented loftier ambitions. Asked how he felt that result would affect the Championship situation, Atkinson, his tongue thrust deep into his cheek, replied: 'I've got to be honest and say that puts us out of it.'

More seriously, he insisted survival was not assured and a slump confirmed the wisdom of his prognosis. Strachan, having announced his retirement from playing at Leeds, ran his 38-year-old legs off in a crucial win over Sheffield Wednesday and reluctantly turned out for the game against Manchester United, a pulsating match. Twice Coventry drew level but a careless back-header by Atkinson's talisman, Kevin Richardson, presented Andy Cole with his second goal and Ferguson's depleted team eventually sneaked through 3–2 to keep the pressure on the leaders, Blackburn, and leave Coventry with work still to be done.

How the strands of football separate and entwine.

L ater that week, there is no obvious sign of foreboding in the Coventry camp. An unseasonal, hot sun beckons the players to the training grounds at Ryton-on-Dunsmore, just round the corner from the sprawling Peugeot plant. Strachan, a tiny, red-headed figure, always busy and inventive as a player, is busy devising some routine, placing markers at the far side of the pitch. Mick Brown, the number two before Strachan arrived, surveys the scene and decides: 'We'll bat first.' There is no shortage of wit here, or the strands of football. Brown and Atkinson go way back and were together, with Strachan, at Old Trafford.

Strachan calls the squad together for a warm-up. A warm-up? It's in the high 70's! They get on with it, Strachan, the little general, leading his troops on a lap of the grounds.

Big Ron appears in the sunlight and you'd swear there is a mutual sigh of appreciation. Judging from the colour of his legs, the weather must have been like this in Coventry for months. He scribbles in large books for a couple of autograph hunters and strolls out to watch as Strachan organises some ball work. He may be 56, the oldest manager in the Premiership, but will he really be saying goodbye to all this and moving 'upstairs' to tend executive matters in two years?

'In two years' time, who knows where anybody will be,' he muses. 'But this arrangement suits me. I think it's a good idea from the club's point of view and it certainly suits Gordon to have two years learning the ropes. I went for Gordon because you look at people you've been associated with in the past, you look at the likes of Bryan Robson, Ray Wilkins and Strachan, and they come into that category of people you know have the right attitude to the game, the right way of conducting themselves. You conclude that they would be logical managers of the future.

'Gordon has officially retired from playing but it's interesting our sponsors made him man of the match the other night. He realises it's needs must at this juncture. It's up to the little fella himself, but if I were him I'd have a little rethink about packing up the game permanently at the top level. He'll certainly be playing a fair amount with the kids in the reserves because he thinks he can teach them something. It might well be, though, that he has some first team games left in him. His fitness level is phenomenal. He's looked after himself, he's trained well, stuck to his diet, all them bananas, and he's got enthusiasm. Hey, and he can still play.'

One of those autograph-seekers had a picture of Atkinson with his Coca Cola Cup-winning Villa team. There is a rumour doing the rounds in the Midlands that you can now get that photograph minus the smiling manager.

Atkinson was not smiling the day Villa's chairman, Doug Ellis, told him his services were no longer required. Villa had always been Atkinson's club. Born in Liverpool but raised in the Midlands, he was an apprentice at Villa Park and although he was to build a playing career at Oxford United, instead, the emotional strands were never broken. His managerial journey took him to non-League Kettering, to Cambridge United, where he somehow achieved promotion from the Fourth Division to the Second in two seasons, to West Bromwich Albion, where he created a flamboyant and feared First Division force, and then to Manchester United. Yet even Old Trafford and Spain could not quite replace Villa in his affections.

'It's no secret it hurt me when I was sacked by the Villa,' he says, in a suddenly solemn tone. 'I knew why it had been done and it had nothing to do with football.'

Ellis, it is said, envied the attention Atkinson commanded. A case of 'this place ain't big enough for the two of us'?

'I think there was a certain amount of that. I've never played politics in football. If you employ me you employ me because you know what I can do with footballers. What annoys me is that certain things have been done by certain people at the Villa to discredit me, and I know full well what's going on. You can call it betrayal. I think somebody's tried to be tricky with me.

'I was angry, though it was not necessarily the lowest point in my career. I was equally angry at Madrid because that was a comic cuts job. In four months we'd gone from down at the bottom to second in the League. Then I get a phone call saying they don't want me. That's Jesus Gil for you. Talk about chairmen. "Mad Max" I used to call him. He came out with all sorts and he's still doing it, but that's what he is. At least he was a character and the daft thing was, I don't think I ever had an argument with him.'

Gil, Ellis, no-one is likely to keep Atkinson down for long. The brash young upstart who used to show off in his £34 Ford Anglia when he was at Villa first time round now runs a Jaguar club car and owns a Rolls-Royce. Still as flash as ever?

'Yeah. Love it.'

He loves everything that goes with his high profile. On a pre-Wembley trip to Majorca in 1983 he suggested a quiet lunch at a little fish restaurant he knew, tucked away in a cove. A couple of glasses of chilled white wine into the repast he was on his feet, giving his rendition of *My Way*. Mick Brown shook his head and said: 'He comes here for a bit of peace but he can't stand it because no-one's recognised him!'

Atkinson willingly plays the role everyone expects him to play. But don't be fooled.

'Hey, I take the thing as seriously as any man in the game,' he stresses. 'But I don't believe you've got to go around with a long face all the time. If you come in and don't enjoy yourself there's no point being in it. My advice to younger managers would be: you have to work hard – and despite what anybody says, nobody puts more into it than me – but at the same time I don't think it's a crime to be seen to be enjoying it. Never have done.

'Losing is the worst part of the game. Getting beat's horrible. It didn't get to me so much the other night [*against United*] because at least we showed a lot of enthusiasm and passion for the game, and although the result wasn't right a lot of people went home saying they enjoyed the game and there's a certain satisfaction in that. What I hate is to see any team of mine cold. I want to enjoy watching my team.

'You can become a bit angry and frustrated on the touchline but you have to accept nobody deliberately makes mistakes and the thing I tell players if they do make a mistake, is just try and rectify it as quickly as possible. If there's a player you wouldn't have expected to make that mistake the other night it's Kevin Richardson but I said okay, you'll probably score the winner on Saturday.

'As a manager, yeah, you make mistakes. There's nobody in the game doesn't make mistakes. But it's all part of the learning process. I have certainly learned. I don't feel there's any problem with a generation gap now between me and the players. Having Strach there might make it easier but I don't feel any different working with players.'

Are you as good as ever you were?

'Better.'

And modest?

'I'm the most modest person I know.'

Could it be that Atkinson's modest playing career, and a couple of years working in a factory, made him a better, hungrier manager? After all, many distinguished players have failed as managers.

'I don't think it makes any difference to a manager what he achieved as a player. It depends on attitude and what your desires are. My playing background didn't make me a better manager. I always say you learn more in the first six months of management than in the whole of your playing career, but I've been in the game 35 years and I've never heard that theory about good players not making good managers till now. It's not only bad players make it as managers – and I was a very good player by the way (*ah!*) – because there are good players who don't do badly as managers.

'Bryan Robson, best player I ever had, without a shadow of a doubt, he's just won promotion in his first year at Middlesbrough and knocked that theory. All the outstanding players I've worked with – Strachan, McGrath, Futre, Whiteside, Muhren and many more I've been lucky to have – had the combination of quality and attitude. You look at all of those, they had the DESIRE to be successful, and that's part of being a great player. It's the same for managers. They can't all be successful, but the good ones have that great desire.'

An outstanding, gifted player being linked with numerous clubs, including Coventry, is Paul Gascoigne, his Italian adventure apparently at an end. Atkinson has no realistic hope of out-bidding the bigger clubs, but he sees an opportunity to flex his club's aspirations.

'The club has a well-appointed stadium, good training facilities, some good players, but I think perhaps what it lacks is something to spark the fans. If we could bring in two or three big name players that the kids could associate with, I can see us getting far bigger crowds. With Gascoigne, I just asked his people to keep us in touch. It would be a swim the Channel job for us because of the number of other clubs involved, but make no mistake, we are ambitious. The club is sound financially and it ain't some sleepy little retreat, you know.'

Not with Big Ron around. It will fizz and the chances are it will have a smile on its face. Without being drawn into the 'good old days' trap he wonders whether relations between current managers are as healthy as they ought to be.

'I do think there has been a bit of a change in attitude sometimes between managers, but I was brought up in an era when there was a big camaraderie. I've always been the same. If other people want to be the other way then that's up to them. If there are any problems with other managers it doesn't worry me, personally, but I'd hate to think camaraderie could go out of the game.

'I reckon we all came into football because we loved playing the game. That's where it started for us, as kids, and we lived the dream. To a certain extent you've got to retain that. Yeah, we've had this about the image of the game and the sleaze and all that, but for every big story – and it's become the popular thing to publicise the negative things and I understand that has to be written about – I just wish we'd give as much space and credence to the good things in the game, because the good things far outweigh the bad.

'I think some of the football this year has been exciting and entertaining. Certainly I would say, and this was something that stood out when I came back from Madrid, there has been over the last few years a greater emphasis on physical power. Even the better teams are very powerful in their approach to the game – the Blackburns, the Man Uniteds. You've got to have the physical input to be able to compete.

'Hey, is it all right with you if I go and do some work now?'

130

He trots on to the pitch, stopping to deliver an encouraging word to one of the young players, and then joins Strachan inside his arrangement of markers. They have a small but captive audience: a few sitting on the grassy bank, one or two leaning on their cars, a man on crutches who still manages to retrieve the ball from beneath a van and a nursery school group who squat in a line and have to listen to Sir's incessant commentary.

Now the boss appears to be involved in the training. Everything around him is a blur of limbs as he shuffles in the middle like a mobile traffic island. 'Not so mobile,' Brown chips in.

They're actually playing pig in the middle. Two pigs in the middle to be precise. Six players have to keep the ball from them using only one touch at a time, and all within the tight confines of Strachan's markers. Big Ron is, you will gather, one of the pigs. Another eight players are operating inside their markers.

Brown chips in again: 'Standard's gone a bit, hasn't it?'

Atkinson agrees: 'Yeah, you're right. Come on, let's lift it. On your toes, nice and bright.'

They abandon the markers, spread across the pitch and go to work practising moves from the back. It's attack v defence. Strachan dutifully takes up his familiar position, wide on the right, as Atkinson orchestrates. The Scot still has his say, though, explaining how Dion Dublin (signed from United) can be used as a decoy, the big striker spinning away to leave space for Peter Ndlovu, the Zimbabwe forward, to dart into. Watching and listening to teams train, you are always struck by the lack of any obvious link with the locality. The player inside Edinburgh-born Strachan has a Scouse accent, the player inside him is a Geordie. It's the same everywhere.

As the bulk of the players make their way back to the dressing-rooms, Atkinson holds back his young Scottish centre-half, Steven Pressley, for heading practice. It was Pressley's failed aerial challenge and tumble which permitted Andy Cole to run on and score United's second goal the other night.

Pressley aborts a leap as he loses sight of the ball. 'Oh, a bit sunny up there, is it?' Atkinson mocks. 'Hey, that Andy Cole didn't stop. He wanted it.'

It's the classic, almost military training procedure. First the rebuke then the praise when the revved up sapper responds.

131

'That's better,' Big Ron enthuses as Pressley powers his header some distance. 'A bit of anger in it.'

Then a bit of classic Atki. Pressley curses at a miserable effort that flops apologetically just in front of him. 'No, you weren't that good,' the gaffer tells him.

They walk off to laughter and you wonder again whether Atkinson could really walk away from this hands-on involvement in the game. He has changed a little, mellowed somewhat. He is more of a homebird. He is settled with his second wife, Maggie, in the Midlands, and on days like this he could be enjoying his pool. On any day he enjoys walking the dogs. But this, working at pitch level, he would miss this, surely?

'You never know in football. I'm not out of the game and I'll be in the game for a long time yet. It's just a question of in what capacity. I mean, let's be honest, if we didn't do well here in two years, they're not really going to want me as manager, anyway. If I do do well, okay, when it's time for Gordon to take over, there's something here for me, or it's a safe bet there's going to be something somewhere for me. I've always got other strings to my bow, so it's a safe bet I'll be involved for a long time yet, in some capacity, in football. I'd be lost without it.'

Would the game be lost without Big Ron?

'You can say that ...'

Pressley comes in for more ribbing in the canteen as he sits down to a plate of pears and grapes. 'Oh, you're not on a fruit diet now, are you?' a team-mate asks. Pressley smiles and eats. There's still more. 'Why did you get all aggressive when you scored the other night?' the teasing team-mate goes on. 'You didn't when you gave them a goal. You went all puppy soft then.' They all laugh and then Pressley tackles a pear.

A lady from the canteen heads down the corridor with a banana. Couldn't be Mr Strachan's lunch by any chance, could it?

A young player can do much worse than emulate Strachan. His self-discipline has enabled him to get extra mileage out of a magnificent career North and South of the border. He has a half century of full Scotland caps and, after Alex Ferguson suspected he was beyond his best, schemed, inspired and cajoled Leeds to the Championship. Even he, however, has now lost his appetite for playing at the top level and the move to Highfield Road has presented him with the opportunity to establish himself in coaching and management.

'As a player, or rather as a coach,' he corrects himself, 'and especially as a father, this gives me a clear picture of what I'm going to do for the next three years, minimum. We've got three children, aged 16, 12 and ten, and this is good for them. I was offered other possibilities but I didn't feel they were as secure as Coventry. They're stable, good people. The club has the potential to do something and that's never really been tapped yet.

'Howard Wilkinson and the chairman wanted me to stay at Leeds, but it was a grey area. Howard could go on for ages yet and I felt a bit of a vulture, hanging about waiting for him to pack in. But this is fine. Everyone knows Ron is going to pack in in two years maybe before that, and that I'm going to be manager after that, so everyone knows where they stand. I've always been friends with Ron, but that wasn't a big part of it. The offer of assistant manager, then manager, was too good to turn down.

'I'm certainly a reluctant player now, aye. I'll play with the reserves. I think I'll be fit enough to do that and at Leeds they thought the young lads came on well when I played with them. But after 23 years of preparing for games, training, travelling in the team bus four hours down to London, listening to rap music, going to my bed in the afternoon, eating pasta for three days, and porridge and all the other things, the way it has to be, it was just getting too much for me. I'd had enough of that. It's easy to switch on for the game against Manchester United and against Sheffield Wednesday, because they were important. But I think this is it now. This is only to try and help Coventry stay in the Premier League. Then it's finished.

'I've been preparing to coach for years, although the gaffer took over today and that's fine because I took a sleeping tablet last night and I still haven't woken up yet. I'm staying at this abbey. There are monks and ghosts all over the place, so I can't get to sleep at night. I'm not a good sleeper at the best of times, so I took a tablet. You get a certain buzz out of coaching, as you do playing, especially if you see people improving, which I did at Leeds. That gave me a great buzz and hopefully I can do the same here.'

Like Robson, he has had eminent tutors.

'I've worked with some great managers, aye, but you couldn't copy one of them because every one of them had his own personality. Big Ron has a bubbly personality, Howard's a bit quiet, Alex Ferguson's fiery, Jock Stein was a man of the world. They had their personalities, I have my personality. You couldn't try and take bits and bobs of every one of them. You'd become a maniac!'

Strachan's services to the game were acknowledged by the PFA, who presented him with a merit award after his official retirement from playing. He took the opportunity to deliver an impassioned defence of English football.

'I wanted to get over that there are a lot of good people in the game and this is why, the longer I am in it, the longer I want to stay in it. The people are good, I like their sense of humour, and they are honest. I'm not saying everyone is as honest as they should be, but 99.9 per cent of them are. You watch German, Italian TV, everyone trying to get each other in trouble. It's great here. I enjoy the camaraderie and I think the football now is the best since I've been in England. The standard is excellent.

'Two things have helped: one, the tackle from behind, when the rule is applied; and two, the pass-back rule of a couple of years ago. They've been good changes and I think the teams at the top of the table reflect that. The only thing that annoys players is inconsistency. If there are rules, fine, we go by them. But sometimes somebody gets kicked from behind and nothing's said. Then somebody can be booked for throwing the ball away. That does annoy players.

'But the product is good, that's why the money's good. Somebody was asking me in Scotland about the sponsorship in England. It's here because the football's good. You cannae sell them rubbish because the sponsors won't be conned. They know. There's a lot of money in the game here. Scotland's suffering because the product there is no good.

'The Premier League has not done anyone any harm and I still think clubs should be going part-time, as well. It's like any job, be it ICI, Peugeot, whatever, if there's things not working in industry they say, "Right, we'll cut back on that." And it should be the same in football. There's teams that have been just existing for 50/60 years. The players would be better off getting a job and playing part-time.

'It's happened in Scotland for a long, long time. You never hear about Scottish teams going to the wall, and most of them are part-time. The Partick Thistles, the St Mirrens, on small crowds, can survive because they pay part-time wages. Players stay part-time rather than join small professional clubs because their wages are good. They get a good wage at the weekend for football and they've got a steady job for the rest of their lives. Some teams are just surviving, hanging on, and some of the players are not getting the national average wage. But they persevere. There may be too many teams.'

It is the quest for security that has sent Strachan to Coventry and meant uprooting the family again.

'They are happy to come down,' he maintains. 'They are ready for a move. It's another adventure in the life of the Strachans. We've been married 18 years and it's great fun. My career's taken me from Dundee to Aberdeen, then down to England and now we're getting further and further South. Might end up at Juventus, eh?'

Strachan was the architect of all Coventry's goals in the 3–1 win at Tottenham, a result which secured the club's place in the Premiership.

CHAPTER 15

Last Edition

David Meek, football reporter

Amid the clamour and near hysteria that has been the Press coverage – in certain sections of the media, anyway – of football's recent past one reporter has been conspicuous not only by his silver hair but also by his stoic determination to maintain the debonair, reasonable, balanced standards of a lifetime. His is the foot-on-the-ball, spray-it-around-thoughtfully style rather than the blood-and-thunder, muck-or-nettles approach, which perhaps explains why he has managed to come through 37 years' covering the affairs of Manchester United to reach 65 and official retirement with his sanity and reputation intact.

Since the dark days that followed the Munich air disaster, David Meek has been the United man at the Manchester Evening News. *Given the club's stature and propensity for incident, it has meant a busy working life. Yet even for United, season 1994–95 at the mercy of Meek's pen has been astonishingly eventful: the then British record £7 million signing of Andy Cole, the Eric Cantona saga and the Roy Keane stamping controversy. All this and another push for the Championship and FA Cup double.*

The ever growing demand for comment and reaction has elevated Meek to celebrity status, and not merely locally. National television has sought his 'expert knowledge' and, in the face of the tabloid mayhem, 'the alternative view'. He is something of a 37-year overnight star.

O ver a cup of coffee in the basement canteen of the *Evening News'* Deansgate building, Meek modestly shrugs off any notions of stardom. 'I think it's just that when the club run into some kind of problem – Cantona, Keane etc – and nobody associated with the club will speak, the next best thing is perhaps the guy who is closest to them and is free to talk. I suppose you do become a sort of spokesman for the club, rightly or wrongly. You appear to give not necessarily the club's views but the club's point of view.'

Meek has football and reporting in his blood, though also a bent for hockey and an unlikely birthright for this job. He is a Yorkshireman.

'I'm originally from York, schooled in York and started work at the York office of the *Yorkshire Post*, where my father had been a journalist, covering York City for 45 years. I did that for two or three years and then went to Australia for a year and worked on papers there.

'While I was there I met Tom Henry, the editor of the *Manchester Evening News* then. When I got back I called to see him and he offered me a job as leader writer and covering politics. I did that for about 18 months, covered a general election in Dublin and Ludovic Kennedy's by-election in Rochdale. Then came the Munich accident in February '58.

'I was in the office that day, just preparing to go home, about four o'clock-ish, when the news came through. The editor cleared the office except for a small team who worked through the evening preparing special editions. I had no connections with the sports desk at the time so I was one of those who went home to follow it as best one could on radio.'

Those killed at Munich included Tom Jackson, who had covered United for the *Evening News* for some 25 years. Meek was deployed to replace him.

'There was apparently nobody free on our sports desk and the editor knew I'd done a bit of sport so I was asked if I would take over on a temporary basis. All the headlines at the time were naturally focused on the players who had been killed and to a certain extent the officials and staff, and of course on Matt Busby and Duncan Edwards, who were fighting for their lives. Sadly, Duncan lost his fight a couple of weeks later. But there were also eight journalists killed. The only writer to survive was Frank Taylor. A photographer and a photographer's assistant also survived.

'I didn't appreciate it at the time but looking back now to those hectic days after Munich I realise that Jimmy Murphy and eventually Matt Busby, when he came back, had to deal not only with the building of a new team, but the problems of building a new media approach because all the people they would have counted as friends had been killed. So there were all these new faces and pieces to deal with and it must have meant yet another little burden at the time.'

Meek had his own burden to bear. 'On the Manchester scene it has always been fairly competitive and in those days we had two evening papers here, so it was a bit cut-throat. If the *Evening Chronicle* had something about United that the *Evening News* didn't have, the old squawk box on the sports desk would go and it would be the editor, who was a great football follower, wanting to know why. So in that sense it was maybe even more competitive than it is now, when we're in competition with local radio and the morning papers.

'When the *Evening Chronicle* merged with the *Evening News* it took that pressure off but the new pressure came in more of a free-for-all, cut-throat tabloid situation. It's less scrupulous now mainly, I think, because newspapers see themselves as having to compete with television, as entertainers. Straight stories are being confined to fewer papers, while more popular tabloids are tending to make more of a circus out of stuff.

'The Eric Cantona affair was a classic example of that, really. The main three – *Mirror, Sun* and *Star* – really did turn it into a circus. They were clearly over the top with the kind of language they used and the readers' polls – "Shall we kick Eric out of England?" and things like that – which wouldn't have been done a few years ago. It all gets hyped up. I think it was the *Sun* who wanted Keane immediately banned from the Cup final. It puts more pressure on me because while I don't think my sports editor would expect me to go to those extremes you get sucked in a bit to compete. I think we had a phone-in: "Should Eric go to prison?" That was in response to the more sensational reports. I couldn't see Tom Henry doing that in the old days. A sign of the times.'

The normal motivation in journalism, as in sport and any walk of life, is to try and reach the top division, the nationals. Meek, who set out resplendent in bow-tie and trilby, the very image of the distinguished scribe, has felt himself adequately sustained at the *News*.

'I did at first wish I'd gone to the nationals,' he says. 'I think Fleet Street burns in the eyes of everybody in journalism. But the truth of the matter is that I was never offered a number one job on a national paper and I always felt that following Man United, albeit for a provincial paper, was equivalent to and maybe more attractive and interesting than being a number three on a national paper.

'In my 37 years United have tended to be always a top team, so that has been my good luck. Even in the Second Division they were pulling in crowds as big as anyone else, they've competed regularly for various competitions and they've travelled regularly in Europe. If I'd been the ultimate ambition man I would have been prepared to take one step back in order to go two forward, but there was never a moment when I wanted to leave Man United because there was always something happening here. It's that sort of club.

'This last year underlines the point. Fancy waiting 36 years before being hit by stories like we've had this season – the £7 million transfer, a stamping incident and Eric Cantona. That sort of thing certainly hasn't happened before. They say there's nothing new in entertainment or newspapers, but it feels like there's been something new this last year. Nothing worse than being bored for your last year and I've certainly not been.

'I've never longed for more or a different team because United have been big enough and in the last few years they've moved from being a football team into something of a much wider, broader stature. They've pioneered the way for so much in the game from years ago, when Matt Busby took them into Europe as the first English club to play in the European Cup. They were the first to have a rights issue of shares, the first, I think, to have the kind of internal takeover we had when Louis Edwards came to power by buying up shares, first club to become a plc, first to merchandise to the extent that United have done. So it has been like changing jobs because so many aspects have broadened my horizons as the club has broadened.'

The danger for Meek and all those journalists who have similar roles is that they get too close to their club and compromise their professional credibility. The club, and those outside, tend to regard them as PR men rather than chroniclers of the truth.

Meek says: 'I try not to see myself as the PR man for United and I think the club unwittingly helped me to achieve that slight independence. In the early 'Seventies, when they sacked Frank O'Farrell, I wrote an article which was headed "Be Fair to Frank". I argued they shouldn't be sacking him, they should be supporting him. They thought I was being deliberately mischievous and obstructive and kicked me off the team coach, or they said I was no longer welcome to travel with them, which is what I had done, as lots of local reporters did, but I think fewer do now. They distanced me, so in a way that made it more professional from my point of view. Having said that, I like to think I've always had a good working relationship with the club and certainly with all the managers, but it's been on a more professional basis than as a pal.

'There have been moments of friction from time to time. When there's such big coverage, as we have on United, you are walking a little bit of a tightrope, trying to be fair to the club and trying to be fair to the demands of the paper, and sometimes one falls off the tightrope one side or the other. You either get a blast from the editor that you shouldn't have concealed that particular piece of information – "look, it's come out somewhere else, we should have had it first" – to going the other way when the club have complained.

'The complaints have been fewer towards the end of my career. Whether that's because they are feeling sorry for my old age, I don't know. I doubt it, though. Sympathy doesn't run through football so much. I think it's more likely that I'm better able to judge how far I can go and what's beyond the limit. But now and again I get challenged as to why I wrote this or that. I think it helps to have come from an era when United had players like George Best, Denis Law and Bobby Charlton, and the other great teams they've had, because when it comes to criticism of a player the modern-day player is well aware that I'm not wet behind the ears and that I've seen some truly great players. Maybe they realise I have a yardstick and are more prepared to accept a critical word from me than they would be if they thought they were the first pros I'd written about.

'When I was younger and maybe because I was younger the players were more ready to have a go for any criticism in the paper. Maurice Setters I remember fondly as particularly vocal, greeting me one day as I got on the coach: "What's that so-and-so crap that was in the Pink?" So you had to stand up to people like him.

'George was okay when you could catch up with him but he was a very young man then and his style of life wasn't quite mine. I got on all right with him but I wouldn't call us friends. Denis I found difficult. He's changed considerably but I think he had a bit of a chip on his shoulder and he didn't take kindly to the media. I remember asking him some questions and he said, "Don't ask me, you do your job, don't get me to do it." I think he just objected to people dissecting him and analysing him and marking him out of ten. There's a certain irony in that he is involved in the media now, giving his comments on radio and so on. His is the most changed personality, I think, of any of those players of that era.

'Also, perhaps, Bobby Charlton. He was a very diffident, shy boy who was a bit – if I put it kindly – happy-go-lucky. You made an appointment to see Bobby and the odds were against his remembering he'd made an appointment. But now, of course, he's a super businessman, jets all over the world, and is a lovely speaker. He can make a speech at the drop of a hat. He's made a huge success of his life, instanced by the fact that it's Sir Bobby Charlton now and he's an ambassador, even representing, I learn, Japan in the Third World.

'I think it is to be admired when people take advantage of the opportunities the life of football brings them. They obviously have that inborn intelligence and get-up-and-go, etc, which have matured. George Best, too. I know he's got his frailties but he's a much more together guy than he was as a youngster. I suppose we all get more assured and confident as we grow older.'

Meek admits he was not a confident young man in the presence of Matt Busby, the founding father of the modern United.

'It took me a long time to get to know Matt because, as I've said, it was a very fraught beginning and when he did come back on the scene it was towards the end of that season and he was a sick man. I was in awe of him. The fact that he had been at death's door made it very difficult to develop a relationship because one was reluctant to pester him. It took time to get closer and he was always a helpful, kind man but I think it took some time before he absolutely trusted me. There was also the *Evening Chronicle* on the go at the time and he didn't play one off against the other. There wasn't the same pressure for news quantity.

'He was like a school headmaster so you wouldn't take any liberties with him. You always had that little bit of respect and when he reckoned you'd written something out of place it was really like being summoned by the headmaster to his study to explain yourself. I never lost that awe of him. It wasn't that he shouted or anything like that. It was just the manner of the man, a presence, and it was that presence, I think, which was 50 per cent of what made him such a great manager.

'I've talked to players of that era and they all felt the same. It wasn't my being particularly diffident. Even the most colourful players, the most forceful players, like Denis Law, felt restrained in the presence of the man. It wasn't because he bawled them out. He talked to them like a Dutch uncle and made them feel ashamed of themselves if they'd done something wrong. Matt had this avuncular style. He called me "lad" until I'd turned 40 so it was rather difficult to get on level terms. But as we both got older we became closer and I'd like to think that for some years before he died we could have called each other friends.'

Meek was to work with some very different Manchester United managers after Busby.

'Wilf McGuinness had 18 months and I don't think he should have been appointed. He should have had better preparation, working with the first team for a couple of years alongside Jack Crompton, but they seemed to think Matt could go on forever. Wilf was out of his depth. He was asked to drop players who were his pals and it didn't work out.

'Frank O'Farrell also had only 18 months. Made a good start but then the old age in the team began to show with cracks and they needed rebuilding. There were too many over-30's in the same team. I think he could have been the right man if they had stuck with him. The legacy of Martin Buchan showed he knew his football. That signing was as good as any. Buchan served United well after poor Frank left.

'With Tommy Docherty it was fast and exciting and he certainly filled the paper with plenty of comments. Looking back, I suppose I was a bit soft with him. I should have exploited him more than I did because he's game to say anything is the Doc and I didn't push him hard enough. Some of the nationals got better stories out of him because they were harder-faced and pushed him into more sensational comments than perhaps I did. So if I've one regret it's that I didn't push him hard enough.

'Dave Sexton was a lovely man but he wasn't tuned in to giving us the media response that we needed in a big newspaper centre like Manchester, revolving round a big club like Man United. So although I count Dave Sexton as a friend, Press-wise he was hard work. He just wasn't really interested in that side, anyway. He wasn't very dynamic. And this showed eventually in the football because it got a little boring, the crowds started to drift away, nothing much was happening and you didn't sense it was going to happen, hence the directors asked him to move over.

'Then they went the other way for a more flamboyant character, Ron Atkinson, who was almost there, I felt. In his five years his team always finished in the top four of the League and twice won the FA Cup, which showed he knew what he was doing. It was just the absence of the Championship that began to bug the directors and they felt that after five years they'd achieved so much but became impatient for the big one. When one or two of his later buys didn't come off they thought it was the end of an era.

'I don't think the break-up of Ron's marriage had any bearing on his departure. His domestic life was outside football. The Doc had gone purely because he ran away or, as he puts it, "fell in love with", the physio's wife. He had to go because a manager and physio must trust each other and work closely together. A lot of us end up in a domestic situation that sees a change but if it's outside the work area it shouldn't make any difference. This unfortunately was within the work area and the Doc had to go. With Ron it was purely a footballing decision. I think maybe they'd got an eye on Alex Ferguson and what he'd done at Aberdeen and that tipped the balance to make the change.

'I get on fine with Alex. From the local reporters' point of view he is a dream to work with. For a start, the mechanics are right. He's at the training ground at half past eight in the morning. We can set our watches by him. I mean, Dave Sexton – and this is not meant as a criticism of him – used to get there at ten to ten and he'd want to be out at five past ten so the local reporters had no chance of getting their information before training.

'Alex has had bust-ups with one or two of the national boys and he's shouted at me from time to time, not, I'm happy to say, so much because of what I've written but because of what has appeared on the news pages of the *MEN*. There can be conflict between what the news desk sees as a suitable story and what the sports desk sees as a story. The news desk thinks the sport department are in bed with United and if they get the chance to show they are independent and fearless they take it, and that upsets the club. Alex took grave exception to a story concerning a visit to the

SAS, which was supposed to be a secret. Alex took the view it endangered the lives of his players and families because, of course, the SAS are not close to the IRA. He flipped and that took a bit of straightening out.'

When you have covered United for so long, seen so many exceptional players, wallowed in so many epic occasions and worked on so many big stories, it is inevitably difficult to condense the highlights, as Meek's attempt to do so proves.

'I reckon the 'Sixties. They won the Cup in '63 with a team that included Noel Cantwell, the captain, Albert Quixall, one of the post-Munich recruits, Johnny Giles, Maurice Setters, Denis Law, Pat Crerand and Bobby Charlton, of course. That was the start of something very exciting and big because also in '63 they were almost relegated. It took another couple of signings and the emergence of George Best to get things to gel and they won the Championship in '65 and '67. So that era was very exciting.

'I was still a relatively young man and you felt you were on the ground floor watching it grow. And the fact that they won the European Cup in '68 was very exciting and very dramatic. Traumatic as well, because to have created the champions of Europe just ten years after having the club wiped out in the air crash was an incredible achievement by Matt Busby. I liked the players in the era – David Sadler, Bill Foulkes, and there was the Charlton-Law-Best trinity. They played together for so long in a settled side.

'But then United have very rarely been boring. Even in the bad times, when they went down to the Second Division, in 1974/75, they were a particularly exciting team. The Doc made wingers fashionable again by playing Steve Coppell and Gordon Hill. I had a lot of time for that team because it was built, not with great sums of money, but by judgment, which I think is the true test of a manager. Nobody particularly rated Steve Coppell, nobody particularly rated Gordon Hill, but the Doc plucked them from the lower divisions and made them into England internationals. I think he was the first to bring back two orthodox, speedy wingers, who took their men on and got in behind them. Their best season was when they came back up to the First Division and made an immediate impact through attacking down the wings.

'Having said all that about the players in the 'Sixties, I think the present squad are a particularly pleasant bunch of guys, though it's harder to get close to them because they're more sophisticated people. There is a bit of an age gap now but I find them very easy to talk to. Steve Bruce is a magic man. When the children are there for autographs, he's the one who can spot a youngster in a wheelchair and goes over to have a word. He's such an affable, helpful sort. Eric Cantona is the most patient, I think, after Steve, of any of the players. The language is a bit of a problem trying to deal with Eric, though I've had two or three conversations where I've felt we were finding a wavelength, but he's a difficult man to get close to.

Of the United players during my time covering them, Eric Cantona is the number two in my books. Number one is George Best. Bobby Charlton and Denis Law come behind them. Eric just has a quality that's very difficult to identify in words. Don't get me wrong, I have every respect for Bobby Charlton, the most graceful player I've ever seen, and Denis Law, the most lethal finisher in the air and on the ground I've ever seen. But Cantona would just edge them because, like George Best, he has that little bit of wondrous magic, the ability to produce the unexpected, and he's a very complete player. The only thing he can't do is tackle – as we've seen! But he's got everything else: two good feet, good in the air, he scores goals, he makes goals and he makes other players play.

'I would defend Alex for the way he's handled and treated Eric. I've heard people say Matt Busby would have booted him out of this country, that he knew how to handle George Best. There is a bit of a myth there. In fact, there's a real comparison in the way Matt bent over backwards with George to keep him playing and Alex has bent over backwards and changed the rules to keep Eric.'

So if Best is number one and Cantona number two, how about picking the Meek United XI, 1958–1995?

'I'd go for Peter Schmeichel in goal. Alex Stepney would be next and Harry Gregg after that. They've all been outstanding goalkeepers and I remember Matt Busby saying that if there was one single factor that edged the Championship for United in '67 it was the signing of Alex Stepney. But I think Schmeichel, the Jolly Green Giant, just has it. When you consider he has gone more than a year without conceding a Premiership goal at Old Trafford that's something.

'Right-back? I'm struggling. Paul Parker, Gary Neville, but I'd probably have to go back to Jimmy Nicholl. Central defenders would be Bill Foulkes and Nobby Stiles, left-back Tony Dunne. Midfield, well, there's Pat Crerand, Bobby Charlton, Paul Ince and you'd have to have Bryan Robson. I'll go for Charlton and Robson, and have four up front. I'd definitely have Andrei Kanchelskis – they've missed him – Law and Cantona in the middle and Best on the left. Ah, and I'd have Denis Irwin at right-back. He can play there. Ince and Crerand would be subs.'

Meek's line-up

	Schmeichel		
Irwin	Foulkes	Stiles	Dunne
	Charlton	Robson	
Kanchelskis	Cantona	Law	Best

No room, then, for the £7million man and Meek admits he has his reservations about Andy Cole.

'I have to say I wonder about his control at times. The ball tends to bounce off him a bit. But you don't score the number of goals he's scored over a period of time without having something. Certainly the five against Ipswich boosted his figures and it's true to say questions are being asked. The luck went on for him at Newcastle. Mark Hughes is always criticised for not scoring lucky goals, just great goals on great occasions. If he has with him a striker who can't play but gets lucky goals you ought to have an effective combination. I think, though, that Cole will be better having Eric in the team, which I am sure is one of the things Alex had in mind when he was trying to make things right for Eric to stay.'

Meek, alas, will not be staying to record their exploits daily for the *Manchester Evening News*, but football, like the hockey pitches – yes, he still plays – and the newspaper trade haven't seen the last of the ever youthful and elegant Yorkshireman.

'I can't bring myself to walk into the sunset,' he says. 'I'm not one to retire to the west coast of Ireland or Cornwall because I think the football in general and Manchester United in particular becomes part of your life and I can't walk away from it completely. I shall continue to go to all the home games and do a bit of freelance work. The editor has asked me to write a weekly column on sport, so I shall also venture occasionally to Maine Road and maybe a few other sports. After all, I'm still an apprentice compared with my father!'

CHAPTER 16

Driven to Win

Alex Ferguson, manager of Manchester United

We must assume David Meek and his cohorts are on European time, or perhaps this is betraying a confidence, but the fact is that Alex Ferguson's Mercedes is parked at Manchester United's Salford training ground nearer 7.30 than 8.30. He works out in the gym, has breakfast with a handful of YTS boys and canteen ladies and is still at his desk long before most office workers, organising his coaches and scouts, and taking calls from the likes of Meek. He was on the phone congratulating Bryan Robson at 8.15 the morning after his former captain's team, Middlesbrough, secured the First Division Championship.

It is a Friday morning, two days before yet another match United have to win to retain any prospect of claiming a third consecutive Premiership. It is a brilliantly clear, bright morning at the Cliff and the training pitch almost opens its arms, inviting you down. YOU could be Charlton or Law or Best down there; or Robson or Giggs or Cantona. Anything seems possible on mornings such as this. Three of those YTS boys are knocking around a ball outside the door, doubtless sharing the dream. Nothing else stirs. In a couple of hours the players will be here for training, the car park will be full and ever-attendant fans will be here for a glimpse, an autograph or a photograph of their favourites. Right now, though, all is quiet and still. Except for the ball being knocked around by the three youngsters.

Just after eight o'clock, and Ferguson strides from the canteen to his office. He looks lean and purposeful. 'Great morning, isn't it?'

Absolutely. Great morning for getting up early and working out.

'I think fitness is important for a manager,' he says, settling into his chair, the pitch forming an appropriate backdrop through his window. 'I think it's important to get your appearance right. When you get to 50 it's more difficult, so you don't want to be doing anything too severe, but you can start off with 20 minutes and build it up, bit by bit. I obviously don't do as much as the players do but it's important to try and keep it up, to care about appearance. It's the same with discipline. I also think discipline is important.'

The rudimentary standards that have carried Ferguson through his prodigious career – his Aberdeen team broke the Celtic-Rangers stranglehold in Scotland and won the European Cup-Winners' Cup before he became United's most successful manager after Matt Busby – were instilled at home in Glasgow. He is as proud of these roots as he is of his achievements in football.

'Aye, it's funny, isn't it? People say you came from a fairly hard background, but when you're young and being brought up you don't see it like that. I never thought that because what you had was what everyone else had. My dad worked in the shipyards and my mother in various factories in the Govan area. He was a shop steward for two or three years and so was I,' recalls Ferguson jnr, who worked five years as a toolmaker and organised a strike over pay.

'The way we were brought up, the things my dad said to us and the driving force he had definitely became inherent in me. When you look back it's strange the things that come to you. My dad always used to call to me and my brother, "Better get to your bed", and we'd sit up laughing, you know, just as lads would. And if we'd come in from dancing he'd say, "Get something in your bellies before you go to bed." Course, you shouldn't eat last thing at night, but that was his great belief and it was part of the sort of upbringing we had. But he made me get to work on time and I realise now the importance of the things he instilled in me.

'I think if you analyse what you need to do well then it is a lot to do with having this driving force within you. It's the self-motivation thing: make sure you are determined and keep going forward, never backwards or sideways. You feel it inside you. For instance, a few minutes after winning a Cup final the adrenalin goes out of me. I've driven myself and now it's gone. I'm flat.

'Some people just have that inner drive. I'm not saying I'm more special than a lot of people that have been successful. I read about Lew Grade, 80 years of age, up and at the office every morning at 6.30. That's the kind of motivating force some have and it becomes a pattern of life for them. Most successful people, whether in industry or sport, have this. I look at managers like John Rudge, at Port Vale. Eleven years he's been doing it there. It needs a certain type of motivation to keep that going when you know realistically there's only so far you can go.

'When people ask about who's going to do it as managers the first thing I look at and ask is: "Could he drive himself when things are really bad?" Bryan Robson is one who has that. He's got the dynamo that makes you keep going, makes you say, "I'll make sure I find a way", you know? There was nothing he couldn't do as a player and nothing he can't achieve as a manager, because of the desire he has. And you use that as an example to your players, that determination to succeed. It's good to see your players go and do well, particularly Robbo because he, probably more than anyone, was instrumental in our success here – on the field and off the field. He was a good guy, that's the first thing, and also he's a marvellous example.'

Ferguson's inner drive was a substantial force behind Aberdeen's ascendency in the face of the Old Firm might, but he applied psychology, too.

'In many ways I dismissed Rangers and Celtic in the minds of the players. I'd been a Rangers player, I'd been on that side of it and seen it. I instilled it into them that there was no reason why it should be a problem. It was a psychological thing with a lot of players, no question. It's the belief factor, competing in every way they compete, that's what it was about. Once we'd established that, there had to be a bit of sophistication about it and that was the next stage. In terms of Rangers and Celtic, we changed the pattern, so that in the end they were trying to beat us.'

He confronted a similar scenario when, after a spell in charge of Scotland, he succeeded Ron Atkinson as manager of United, in November, 1986. The seat of power in the English game was Merseyside.

'Liverpool was certainly the main target,' he says, 'though for a spell Everton were up there too. The Liverpool of that time was a really good side. But Arsenal helped in a way because they won two titles in the period that followed, so things started balancing out. Gradually we were hearing less about the Liverpool system, this invincibility. They've not won the Championship for five years now and there's been a more even spread, but we obviously hope to go on and dominate the way Liverpool did.'

United's elevation has done nothing to improve relations with Liverpool. Ferguson sampled the ill-feeling when he first went to Anfield as United's manager. Abuse from the home dressing-room took him aback. So did comments to be expressed by the then manager, Kenny Dalglish. The Scot with the Celtic background reckoned his baby daughter had more sense than the former Ranger. The enmity between them has added spice to the contest for supremacy against a Blackburn Rovers managed by Dalglish. Those strands again.

'Yeah, it did shock me at the time,' Ferguson says, in barely a whisper. Suddenly the feared 'Taggart'-like persona melts. He seems gentle and sensitive. 'I think possibly there has been a bit of envy regarding Man United and I'm going back before my time and only on hearsay, things I've picked up. But there does seem to have been a bit of envy from Liverpool, the fact that they were winning the titles and United were still getting the headlines and the biggest crowds. It's a strange, strange thing.

'I remember Graeme Souness [*a player and later manager at Liverpool*] wrote when he went to Rangers that they, Rangers, were the second biggest club in Britain after Manchester United. That tells you a story because he was a great Liverpool player. I have thought about this, the bad feeling between the clubs and in many ways our supporters reciprocate that sort of hatred.

'But having been here eight and a half years, you get to understand the nature of supporters and what they're about. The one thing you have to say about Liverpool supporters is they do appreciate good football. I think if we were to go there the last game of the season and win the League it might be different, but afterwards they would hold up their hands and say, "Yeah, United were the better team, they played great football."

'Our players have been abused at lots of grounds this season, and we've had to look at our security. You arrive at grounds and there are kids at the front who have waited for autographs but the players can't stop because of the abuse and the spitting from behind. We have seen other instances of bad crowd behaviour surface again and we can only hope it's just another passing phase.'

But Dalglish?

'I don't know where a lot of that stuff comes from,' he insists. 'I don't understand that. There's always going to be people putting a side on things. A lot of them are more concerned with selling newspapers than telling the real story. I don't think there's really bad blood between managers. You will always get on with one person better than another, simply because of your culture or your age, that type of thing.

'When I came down here, taking over from Ron, people maybe thought we wouldn't get on, simply because I took his job. But I always found Ron really good and we get on without any bother, and I think that's how it is with most of the managers. We can have a drink together, no matter what. We always invite visiting staff to our office after a game and get the same treatment at most grounds we go to.'

Ferguson is regarded as a prickly recipient of criticism, though he contends he is more philosophical these days.

'I don't really read the papers, to be honest with you. We have a legal side that looks at everything, to check for libel and that sort of thing, and Ken Ramsden [*the club's assistant secretary*] will scour the papers and give us a briefing on what's been said. But you know the journalists who are always looking to have a pop at the club.'

United are particularly aggrieved over the Eric Cantona and Roy Keane affairs. The club consulted with the FA after Cantona's kung-fu attack on a foul-mouthed Crystal Palace fan and suspended him for the rest of the season, conscious that would undermine their Championship prospects, only for the authorities to extend the ban until the end of September. Keane, dismissed for stamping on an opponent on the night Ferguson and Palace's manager, Alan Smith, called for calm in the wake of a Palace supporter's death, was charged with bringing the game into disrepute, a move which threatened his place in the FA Cup final team. United felt that in both instances the FA bowed to media pressure.

'I definitely think we were unfairly treated over Cantona and Keane,' Ferguson says. 'It makes me laugh when people go on about all the so-called incidents our players have been involved in this past year and you see some of the tackles that go on in other games. There's not been one broken nose, broken jaw, cut, gash, knee ligament injury or even a bled wart, not a flippin' thing as a result of our players' tackles.'

Fair point, but perhaps if Ferguson or Cantona had been more apologetic in public, more sympathy might have been forthcoming.

'No chance of that,' Ferguson responds firmly. 'I don't think there was any thought in my mind other than that the jury was out. I have no doubt we were betrayed by the FA. I don't think there's a strong leader down there. I think there's a situation where they are dominated by the Press. They listen more to the Press than the people in the game. We spoke to the FA about the Cantona situation. Negotiations were going on. There were at least half a dozen phone calls in the course of the night between the chairman [*Martin Edwards*] and the FA.'

Cantona also found himself in court, charged with common assault. He was found guilty and given a jail sentence, but on appeal that was amended to 120 hours' community service, imparting his (football) skills to youngsters. Ferguson, meanwhile, was striving to keep the player from the clutches of Internazionale of Milan and other interested clubs, and eventually the Frenchman agreed a new, three-year deal with United. That, Ferguson contends, vindicates his handling of Cantona.

'Eric wants to stay and that's the important thing. If we had put him on the transfer list, how many English clubs do you think would have been interested? A few, I would reckon. He's a marvellous player. He's integrated into the team really well. He gets wound up in the dressing-room by Paul Ince the way everybody does. The players respect him and appreciate what he does.

'I have been criticised for being too protective of Eric, but we protect anybody at this club who has a problem. If they've stepped out of line in any way we deal with it, though not in the public sector. We feel it should be dealt with in here. And the players keep it within the club. I'm sure a lot of our boys could walk out of the dressing-room and sell their own story about a certain player being disciplined, or how we run things or maybe what I've said about Eric, but none of them have, so I've got great respect for the lads. I do believe we have a bond here.

'You can't keep punishing someone forever. You hope they learn. You hope it's the last time. In the case of Eric, I think it would be the last time, because the pressure on him will be enormous. He is an emotional player on the pitch but he has a wealth of experience and he feels he can handle it. I think he can. I think he'll get stick, but he's always got stick because he's such a great player.

'He's given great moments. People come to watch him play. We can't accept one or two things that he's done and we tell him not to tackle because he's not a good tackler. We try to teach him to get into positions where he's a defender, where he comes behind the ball, and he does that quite well. We hope the ban will have a tremendous impact on the lad. He's effectively out till November because it will take him four or five games to get back. People don't understand that a centre-forward's career is usually over at the top level by about 32 or 33, and Eric is 29, so it has hit him hard.

'Fortunately, Eric's also a marvellous trainer. Some players dedicate themselves to training, to improve themselves, and that's why they last so long. Mark Hughes, Brian McClair and Steve Bruce are all good trainers, good pros. Jesper Olsen was a terrific trainer. Gordon Strachan was always a great pre-season trainer. He'd do the long runs, no problem at all. It's maybe easier for Manchester United to have players who will train well because it's such a big club and if they want to stay in the mainstream they have to keep it up.

'You'll see one or two slip back in terms of training performance and eventually they'll slip away. That happens all the time at this club, even at younger levels. The job you don't want is to tell a player he has no future at the club. But nobody else will do that. You have to. It's the same every year, some have to go. It's tremendously satisfying, though, when you see kids come through. We've put a lot of work into our youth system here and we've got to the final of the FA Youth Cup again this year. We have two or three decent young players.

'There are different ways of managing. Going back to Liverpool, way back they bought their players. Now they've had to change, still buying younger players to develop, such as James and Redknapp, but bringing on more of their own young players, like Fowler and McManaman. Brian Clough, in his early years at Forest, bought all his players. I think it was said he didn't believe in young players. Then he had a barren spell and went to a youth policy. We've brought through a lot of young players who have made a career out of the game, whether here or elsewhere.'

A number of the young players still at Old Trafford have been deployed by their beleaguered manager in pursuit of a second consecutive double. The Championship victory of 1993 was the first by United in 26 years and of obvious significance, yet a title this time would, Ferguson argues, be more satisfying still.

'Winning the League for the first time with United was definitely the high point for me,' Ferguson says, 'because that was the catalyst, really. That settled everyone down. The supporters lost their anxiety. But it would be the greatest triumph this club ever had if we won it this time, considering all the injuries and suspensions we've had and all the media attention we've had. It would be an incredible performance. In fact, no matter what happens, they've been fantastic. To stay in there and keep it going right to the wire, the way they have done, has been unbelievable. It's been character and experience, and the kids have played their part superbly. There is no fear with them, you see. They just go out and play.'

The landmarks of the 'Nineties are a far cry from the low point of Ferguson's career, when he seriously wondered whether he had lost his way. Now he readily locates the period.

'It was December, '89, before we started to pick up and had that Cup win against Forest. I think you maybe analyse more when you are in that situation, and deep down you worry. I'm no different to anyone else. I was a little concerned. "Am I doing the right thing?" you ask yourself. "Is the training right, have I picked the right team, is the package right?" You think all these various things. And I felt that we were going the right way, but what I needed was a bit of luck. I had that at the Forest game with the Mark Robins goal. The supporters were not going to accept we were out of the Cup, they were magnificent, and the team were inspired.

'I didn't think I'd be able to pick a team that day, because there were so many players out. I took everyone to the game that day and in the stand we had six internationals, all injured. But in the end all of them, Robson and the rest, were really chuffed, you know? That was the start. When we won that game, everybody thought we were going to win the Cup. The supporters were excited, and watching the acceleration of expectation, getting bigger and bigger with each game, was terrific.

'We had to go to Hereford, horrible pitch, and won 1–0. Great game at Newcastle, 3–2. The excitement was unbelievable. And

then that terrific semi-final against Oldham. So it was a really exciting Cup run and eventually winning the Cup against Palace helped
the players overcome a lot of doubts about whether they were good
enough to play for Manchester United. They were quite young at
the time but they grew up after that.'

The following season United won the European Cup-Winners'
Cup – emulating the much-acclaimed feat of Ferguson's Aberdeen –
and were runners-up in the League Cup. In 1992 they won the
League Cup and were runners-up in the Championship, capitulat-
ing at the last to Leeds United, Cantona, Strachan and all. They
were emphatic winners of the inaugural Premier League
Championship in '93, and defeat at the hands of Aston Villa in the
'94 League Cup final denied them a unique domestic treble that season.

This 1994–95 campaign has been more problematical. United
have lost some of their fluency and consistency, along with key personnel. Eliminated from the Champions' League and Coca Cola
(League) Cup, they paid a British record £7 million for Newcastle's
Andy Cole. He was ineligible for the FA Cup but his five goals in
the 9–0 annihilation of Ipswich Town sustained the Premiership
objective. Compensating for the absence of Cantona, however, was
another matter. Almost as damaging has been the injury to Andrei
Kanchelskis and the winger's apparent rift with Ferguson.

'It's a strange one,' the manager says, genuinely puzzled. 'I can
only think he's been got at. Players don't usually ask to leave
Manchester United. The last was Paul McGrath. We have rotated
players and changed the team depending on circumstances.
McClair, Hughes, Giggs, Bruce, Sharpe, Irwin, Keane – they've all
been left out on occasions. They don't like it but they don't react. I
left Andy out at Chelsea because the pitch was ten yards narrower.
In the event, he came on and did well.'

At this late stage of the season Ferguson no longer has the luxury of being able to rotate players. The irony is that Kanchelskis,
said by his agent not to get on with Ferguson, would now be an
automatic and vital choice. The 53-year-old manager appears to
have taken this and other setbacks with uncharacteristic restraint.

'I can still have a temper but I think people do mellow with
age,' he says. 'You tend to observe more as you grow older. It's a
great asset to acquire, I believe. I observe more than I ever did.

Whether it's maybe in my management style over the years, the hands-on involvement, or whatever, I've tried to step back and observe a lot more. I think watching people and their habits is important. It gives me a better insight into what makes them tick, how to use them, how to handle them in the right way.

'I'm able to step back because I've got good staff here, right the way through the club. Brian Kidd has been magnificent to have alongside me. He's been fantastic for this club. His heart's in the club but also he's dedicated to the job he's doing. He's loyal to me and his commitment to the players is great. His training sessions are excellent. He takes a lot of care and consideration over his training.'

More mellow he may be, but totally fulfilled he is not. The driving force generated in Govan demands of him one more big effort, one more achievement.

'The European Cup has to be the main target for this club again. We don't want it to become an albatross for us but it has to be the aim. But there's no way I look to a new challenge beyond United. When I finish here I feel sure that will be it. I can't see anything greater than this.'

That final ambition will have to wait at least another year. United lost the Championship to Blackburn by one point, West Ham resisting their pressure to hold out for the decisive 1–1 draw on a tense and enthralling last afternoon of the season. Ferguson's depleted team also yielded the FA Cup, losing 1–0 in the final against Everton. They have the consolation of a place in the UEFA Cup and the next generation of players won the FA Youth Cup, but the sale of Paul Ince to Internationale and Mark Hughes to Chelsea dismayed supporters. Eventually Andrei Kanchelskis went, too, to Everton.

CHAPTER 17

Spirit of '66 and All That

Alan Ball, manager of Southampton

To a certain generation, Alan Ball will always be the little red-head, running himself into Wembley's verdant pastures. There was Bobby Charlton, ever flowing, ever explosive; Bobby Moore, elegant and imperious; Gordon Banks, simply the best long before the song; Ray Wilson, master of the full-back trade; George Cohen, marauding on the other side; Big Jack Charlton, redoubtable and ... big; Nobby Stiles, respectfully called 'The Bad One' by Portuguese supporters; Martin Peters, supposedly ten years ahead of his time; Geoff Hurst, the hat-trick man who made sure it was all over; and Roger Hunt, the self-effacing alternative to Jimmy Greaves. But if anyone embodied the spirit of England that sun-blessed afternoon in 1966, it was the 21-year-old Blackpool player destined for Everton. Bally's effervescence sustained the cause and his cross led to that dubious third goal against West Germany, tilting the World Cup final England's way.

The spirit would be evident throughout the rest of his playing career. He went on to earn 72 international caps. After winning a League Championship medal with Everton, he joined Arsenal, and from there he went to Southampton, captaining Lawrie McMenemy's promotion side of 1978. He dipped his toe into the perilous waters of management as player-boss of Blackpool before a second spell at Southampton and a final fling with Bristol Rovers.

It was 1984 and time to dive into the deep end of management, back down on the South Coast, though with Portsmouth. Within three years he had guided them to the First Division, but could not keep them there and departed in '89. The spirit would not be broken and he worked his way back through jobs at Colchester, Stoke and Exeter. The spirit was even deployed, briefly, in an attempt to bolster England again.

On the face of it, he was presented with an equally improbable objective midway through the 1993–94 season – to preserve Southampton's Premiership status. The club had been unable to hold its best players, attendances were modest and plans for a new stadium appeared to be getting nowhere. But ... Lawrie McMenemy, as 'director of football', would be there to lean on if necessary, Matthew Le Tissier was still at The Dell and, much as he was engrossed in, and emotionally rewarded by, his work at Exeter, this was a challenge Ball could not refuse.

Management has proved beyond the wit, patience and motivation of the majority in England's World Cup-winning team. Big Jack is a notable exception yet as perhaps the least gifted player that may not be a coincidence. His brother, Bobby, for instance, the most gifted in the team, had an ill-starred stint as manager at Preston. His players at the time confided that he could not understand why they were incapable of responding to his requirements. 'The fact is that he is still twice as good as any of us,' said one, 'but it comes naturally to him. It doesn't to us.'

Ball was determined to find a way. It was time to roll down the socks and run and scrap and probe, just as he had done that sun-blessed afternoon in 1966. He kept Southampton up and has done so again. What's more, he has done it in a manner befitting this humble yet dignified bastion of football's finer qualities.

I t is a sun-blessed morning in 1995 and Ball has returned to Southampton's Cheshire hotel after supervising a light training session ahead of the team's match at Everton. He is chunkier now and doubtless unable to cover the ground he could. His voice is less squeaky. But he still has a full head of red hair and he still bustles with positive, infectious intent. He is relishing this return to Goodison Park, the chance to show off his side. They are free from the threat of relegation. Everton are not.

Whether or not the spirit of '66 is back to haunt Everton, the subject of his England contemporaries is never far from his mind.

'I know exactly why so many of them didn't do well in management,' he says with no need for consideration. 'It nearly happened to me. The simple reason is your own standards. You cannot tolerate people who are not prepared to work at their game to reach those standards, you cannot tolerate people who haven't got the same ambition as yourself and finally it's difficult to tolerate people who don't have the same ability as you had. Put all those together and you begin to understand. I've asked myself many-a time, "What am I doing here trying to help these players to play when they can't even help themselves?" It is that tolerance level that you can't come to terms with. You can't understand why people don't set themselves the standards you set yourself.'

Ball presumably did understand, did come to terms with the dilemma and found a way round it. But how?

'I got round that purely by necessity. I needed a job and I told myself I couldn't let that beat me, so I went back to basics and said, "Right, I will try to produce kids to do the things I want to do." I started at Portsmouth and I was very much a tomorrow manager. It cost me my job at Stoke because they wanted a today man and I was still a tomorrow man. Although it backfired on me there I decided I still needed to go back to basics, to go back to the kids and build belief in the game; in myself, really.

'I love my football. I love teaching if people want to learn. I don't tell them, "What I say you do", I ask them, "Can you do it?" There's a subtle difference there and if they can do it, I'll say, "Right, I'll give you more to do and more to do until I've helped you be as good as you want to be." That's been my philosophy. The knack is the development of what is there, asking them to do things. Sometimes they might not be able to do it, sometimes they might not have the desire to do it, the passion to do it, and you've got to find that out very quickly. You can't help those people go very far. But if they have the ability and the desire, you can give them other things that can help them go a long way.'

Ball's aim is to take the players of Southampton a long way and have them rocking in the aisles down at The Dell.

'Southampton is certainly not a sleepy haven when I'm there,' he says. 'I've made them aware of what they can achieve and what they can do. We're running to full houses now. Wherever you go in the theatre, if you're running to full houses you can run for years because you're doing something right. We've survived this year, which has been a really tough year with four going down, but we've played football everywhere we've been. We've scored 60 goals, we've been involved in fantastic games and for a little club that's great. We've got an awful lot of plaudits from people.

'That's the way we've gone about handling this fraught season. We've been up front. There's no point in hiding things from people. What you see is what you get, whether you like it or not. It's entirely up to you. That's the way my dad brought me up. Managers have been going all over the place this season because of

159

the relegation system and people panicking. It's been the worst in the history of the game. I've thought to myself, "Boy, this is the year you stand by your principles, and your players and your supporters will admire you for that – and you can admire yourself for that. You've got to find yourself. Can you handle it? Can you hack it? Are you strong enough to believe in playing football and go and try to entertain away from home?"

'I was paid a lovely compliment by Roy Evans at Liverpool the other week. We got beat 3–1 but he said, "No team's come here and played as open a game as that for years and years. Good luck to you, I hope your beliefs are right." That was the one game we lost in a run of eight. We won six and drew one. As I went home on the coach I thought about what Roy had said and it gave me a lot of heart.'

Ball is honest enough, however, to acknowledge the threshold of success can vary from club to club.

'I think I can gain as much satisfaction from what I've done as those at the top and I think if you talk to Alex Ferguson and Kenny Dalglish they will agree with that. But in many ways they've got bigger jobs because of what is expected of them. Success at that level is not expected of Southampton. It's nice if it happens for Southampton, but they are living on another planet concerning pressure because they've got to do it. That's the subtle difference. That's where it's hard for them. But again, I've got to produce young players, I've got to buy very well, and I've got a genius who's already there, which has helped me an awful lot.

'This lad has been absolutely fantastic for me and it makes me mad when people don't understand why I champion this lad's cause, why I pester Venables to play him. They must understand that this lad has been virtually everything for me. My first two or three months here, he kept this club in the division. This year other people have done it as well in a team situation. But he's been magnificent again. He's been loyal as anything for this club and I just think he deserves his manager backing him to the hilt.'

For the benefit of those living on yet another planet, it should be explained that this genius of a lad is Le Tissier, and it is fair to assume everybody bound for Goodison Park this afternoon is looking forward to seeing his performance.

'He won't be playing,' Ball says, apologetically. 'He's injured. I've just given him a fitness test. Last two games he's played his heel has been really sore. He shouldn't have played last Saturday. He definitely shouldn't have played the other night. He finished very lame. He hasn't trained all week. Listen, I wanted him to play here today, to show people what he can do, but I can't risk him.'

Back to England and Terry Venables' resistance to Ball's entreaties.

'I don't know why Terry doesn't trust him. When Terry wants to tell me he will do, I suppose, but I'm not going to ask him. I just keep pestering him, telling him he's wrong. I've no theories, I haven't got a clue. He's the best, in my opinion, in the country. Football's all about opinions. I won't tell Terry how to do his job, I'll just pester Terry and drive him mad. He'd do the same if he had a player like that. If you switched the roles he'd be doing the same to me. With his absolutely fantastic ability, the lad would have been able to handle the '66 squad, and the '70 squad, without a shadow of a doubt. The boy is special, believe you me, special.'

Many are still puzzled, though, that a player so special should not crave a grander stage.

'At Southampton he is very happy,' Ball counters. 'Happiness is a big thing in life, you know. When you find it, why chance throwing it away? He's very well paid and he's signed for three years. He's absolutely worshipped where he is. He's very close to his family, who live on Guernsey, and he can get there with ease. He's very much a family-orientated person and he just seems to me to be a very contented 26-year-old. People talk about ambition and this, that and the other, but he has played for his country and if I can become the manager they and I want me to be, then we can get a team here capable of winning things. That's my ambition and he knows that. He also knows my feelings about him and he's prepared to put his ten penn'orth in with me, which is lovely.

'The other players don't resent the praise I give him. We got that out of the way straight away. I told them he was the best player in the club, I told them he's the best player in England, I told them he's maybe the best player in Europe. Now the pressure's on him. Within a team framework, we play in such a way that we use him in areas where they've got to get the ball to him and then he has to produce. Which he's done.

161

'The others don't get upset. You can't not like this boy. He's the loveliest lad in the world and I think they're all his friends. He's not arrogant. He's arrogant with the ball but he's not arrogant as a person and listen, he helps them with bonuses and they help him with bonuses. You've only got to look at his stats. I don't think Venables would take a different view if the lad had been with Man United or some other club. That's neither here nor there as far as I'm concerned.'

If Le Tissier has no overt desire to flex his skills with a bigger club, how about Ball?

'I don't even think about what I could do with a bigger club,' he maintains. 'Not at this moment in time. The important thing for me is myself and I am always asking myself questions. I'm always asking myself what I can achieve, where can I go with the players I have. I took this job on 18 months ago after having a wonderful time at Exeter. Believe it or not, I was very happy there. I was given time to produce kids there and I was halfway through it. But when the phone call came with the offer to manage a Premier League club, all the questions came flooding back: "Can you do it? Do you think you're good enough? Can you hack it, son? This is your chance. If you don't make a good job of this you'll go down in history as not a bad player, yes, someone who's brought kids up, the Darren Andertons of this world, yeah, you could do that, but you couldn't manage a top side."

'At this moment in time I'm doing all right but I've still got questions to ask myself. I'm very, very hard on myself. I'm as hard as my dad would be on me if he was still alive. That keeps me right because I'm very ambitious. My dad is still there, really. He was a real football man and I'm just wondering what questions he'd ask me or what he would demand of me, and I try to put them into my own thoughts on where I want to go to the point of being frightened of failing.'

Irrespective of Ball's success or otherwise as the manager of a Premiership club, he will always be one of the Chosen XI, the heroes of '66.

'People still stop me and talk to me about '66. There isn't a day goes by that it's not brought up. There isn't a day goes by without that third goal being discussed. I don't think it will ever go away. All I can say is that Roger Hunt's reaction, as the ball comes down from the underside of the bar, is the reaction of a player who believes it has crossed the line. But I couldn't tell whether it was in or out, and

I crossed the ball for Geoff Hurst and I was in a really good position. The Russian linesman had no chance of seeing it but it counted, anyway.

'To be the best in the world at anything, for a country as small as this, is wonderful. It happened when I was too young, I suppose. A lot of it went over my head. I didn't appreciate what was happening. But the fact that people ask you every day of your life about it, and it's coming up to 30 years since it happened, it just shows how big it has become.

'I just wish people would do a little bit more for us. I think we've had about three reunions. I think maybe a couple from the squad may have fallen on hard times. The 25th anniversary would have been the perfect opportunity, but nothing was done. The 30th . . . perhaps? The eve of the European Championship, maybe? But that's typically English, isn't it? We are shocking when it comes to caring for our own. I just wonder how Alf is, you know? The powers that be should be looking into that. Everybody goes on about what a fantastic thing it was, but what's happened to all those lads?

'I think we got £1,000 for winning the World Cup. Harold Wilson's supertax meant we brought home about £475. For being the best in the world for your country. Four hundred and seventy-five pounds! Do me a favour. I mean, you're talking millionaires now and they're not playing at that level. Surely some sort of recognition can be made. I can honestly say I've never been offered a Cup final ticket, I've never been offered a seat to an international by the FA since that day. And it's the same for the other World Cup players.

'That's only a small thing. We should be ambassadors. Pele is, Eusebio is. There are so many of them around, household names. Bobby Charlton does a bit, but more for Manchester United. Ray Wilson, Gordon Banks – these are big names, but we're not used properly. We underplay our heroes. Imagine if you were an American in that situation. If you'd been the best in the world for America you'd never want for anything in your life, but not this country.'

Ball's achievement in taking Southampton to tenth place in the Premiership's final standings for 1994–95, the club's best finish in the top division for five years, was recognised with the offer of an extended contract, but he chose to join Manchester City.

CHAPTER 18

Sky's the Limit

Andy Gray, Sky television commentator

Apart from the proliferation of all-new, all-seater stadia, nothing is more readily associated with the modern game than the near saturation coverage given by Sky Television. The satellite channel has not only landed on England's – and Scotland's – playing fields, lavishing gold and feel-good, it has also dragged its terrestrial rivals, however reluctantly, towards the next millennium.

Critics of Sky's approach complain of too much talk, too much analysis, too much hype, too much interference with fixtures, too much everything. They also grumble it costs too much. Traditionalists contend Sky's football is more circus than sport, and certainly they were close to that with the dancing girls and fireworks that accompanied the early Monday evening presentations. But subscribers, in increasing numbers, have demonstrated an apparently insatiable appetite for this all-embracing show. After all, football fans love talking about the game as much as watching it. The talk and the play-backs go on through the week; there are previews and reviews; there are forums and tactical insights. Every conceivable angle and opinion is considered.

Sky has endeavoured to breathe new life into televised football and, like it or loathe it, you would have to admit they have achieved that. It is vibrant, even brash, sometimes over the top. But it is alive. With Andy Gray in the front-line it would have to be. The enthusiasm he carried on to the pitch he now lifts up on to the gantry. As a striker he was always prepared to go in head-first and he is no less combative as Sky's resident co-commentator, sitting alternatively alongside Martin Tyler and Ian Darke.

Gray fits perfectly the requirements for Sky's 'expert' pundit. He had a distinguished playing career with Scotland and a number of clubs, mainly south of the border, he's chirpy and always talkative. He moved from Dundee United to Aston Villa and returned to Villa Park after spells with Wolves and Everton. He had a swansong with Rangers and later yet another stint with Villa, this time as assistant manager to Ron Atkinson. By, then, however, he was already part of the satellite revolution and eventually he opted for the box full-time.

It is approaching 4 o'clock on a Monday afternoon, some four hours before the start of the Blackburn Rovers-Newcastle United match, and groups – nae, hordes – of technicians are standing around, chatting, in the encampment of vans behind the new main stand at Ewood Park. Do they really need all this manpower? Seemingly so.

Ian Darke, the Monday man, shuffles across the road, through a side gate and into the ground. Perhaps to take a look at the pitch, perhaps just to get a feel of the place. It's his match, also, remember. Up in that new main stand – the Jack Walker Stand, of course – programme presenter Richard Keys is running through his introductory script with his producer. Gray is sitting in on the rehearsal but jumps to his feet and spins round to peer down onto the playing area when a figure saunters into shot.

'Get off the pitch, you hooligan, Darkey,' Gray bellows. Darkey is, by now, accustomed to Gray's ribbing, and he can expect more on air.

It has been the proverbial long, hard season for the Sky crew, too, yet there is an ebullience in the studio which is a tribute to their stamina. They are into the last week of the Premiership season but there is every prospect of a final day decider and Sky Sports, utilising both their channels, are preparing to screen the crucial final fixtures: Liverpool versus Blackburn and West Ham versus Manchester United.

'Oh, I hope it goes to that,' Gray says as we slip out of the studio, into a spacious restaurant which overlooks the pitch. 'We've not had that yet. It will be great.'

The enthusiasm is remorseless. Surely, though, it was a difficult decision to divert that enthusiasm away from a direct involvement in the game?

'It was an easy decision because I was virtually unemployed,' he replies. 'When I left Rangers I came back down to the Midlands and sat about waiting for the phone to ring and wondering what, at 33 and a bit years of age, I might do. It didn't ring very often but one call I did get was to ask me if I was interested in joining a team being put together for the old satellite station, BSB. I liked their ideas and was quite excited with being in at the beginning of something. For two years we worked quite hard and then the merger happened between Sky and BSB, and I did a year with Sky as well as managing. Ron asked me to be his assistant at Villa, which I did and loved every minute of it, but it was too hard doing both jobs. I didn't have a day off from August to May.

'So then when Sky secured the Premiership contract they were going to be asking more and more of me. The chairman was concerned I was doing too much television work anyway so I had to make a decision. It wasn't a difficult one, much as I loved working with Big Ron and working with the players. My basic enjoyment was playing the game. All I'd ever wanted to do was play football. The television offer was a good one, I'd enjoyed the work and the decision was not as difficult as many people have imagined.

'I didn't see myself in management then and I still don't. Everything being equal, I'd like to think my future lies in television but you never say never. Things may arise, situations might change. I've often wondered how good a manager I might have been and lot of people tell me they think I've got the qualities that would have made a good manager, but you never know until you try. I don't think I could drop down to the Third or Second Division, managing on a shoestring. I never knew what it was like to play there so I've no experience of that, but I certainly would have fancied getting in somewhere like Villa or Everton or Wolves, where I played, big clubs where you could actually do something.'

Instead, he is with Sky, giving the established television channels a hard time. Even a kick up the backside?

'I think the Beeb and ITV have covered sport really well,' he opens with measured diplomacy, 'but Sky have covered football the way the public have always wanted to see football covered. Before, they basically got what they were given: this is the way it is, end of story. We've listened to the public, given them what they want and given football a platform it's never had. And we've given it financial backing it's never had [*A £304 million deal*]. And yes, if you like, we have given the BBC and ITV a kick up the backside.'

That's more like it, Andy.

'I think we've shot the game forward an awful lot in three years. The way we cover it, the time we give it, was unheard of before Sky. We have an hour's build-up on a Sunday and again on a Monday. It's normally five minutes: "Hello, good evening and welcome, here's the match". We build up every match we cover and supplement the football with magazine programmes – *The Bootroom*,

The Footballers' Football Show, *Sky Soccer Weekend*, *Goals on Sunday*. With all these programmes, football's never had a higher profile than it has now.'

Some would argue this profile comes at too high a price, that the tail is wagging the dog, that too many fixtures are being moved around, and that too many matches are given rave reviews they do not merit.

'I would disagree,' Gray says firmly. 'Games were moved around long before Sky came on the screen. ITV's games were always on a Sunday. The major change we have made is on Monday night and I think Monday night games have now become an institu-ion. It's become part of the football calendar, a bonus, and football supporters would miss it if it wasn't there. I think players enjoy it, fans enjoy it and certainly armchair fans love it. Yes, when it gets near the end of the season and the Championship is about to be decided we want, with all the investment we've put in the game, to be there at the end. What other channel would go out there the last day of the season and give you two live games, at the same time, so supporters all over the country can see them?

'The second criticism about the game not being as good as we may say: well, I love the game, I try to pick out the better things in the game, but I don't sit up there and say to the public, "This is wonderful", when it's crap. I believe football supporters know more about the game than many people give them credit for, so I would never dream of doing that. I think that's an unfair criticism, cer-tainly of me, and an unfair criticism of anyone else here. I've cov-ered many bad games and said they were bad.

'Anyone can sit up there and say this is hopeless, but to sit up there and say why it might be bad – is it because the players are poor, or is it because they are passing the ball badly, is one team doing quite well at stopping the other team playing? – that's what I try to do. The game yesterday was a classic example, Man United versus Sheffield Wednesday. It wasn't a good game at all. Wednesday were ordinary and United did what they had to do, they won the game. I don't think the criticism stands up.

'The other criticism of Sky is the saturation. Yes, we do show an awful lot of live football. I don't imagine everybody watches every live football match, but what we're giving the football public is a choice. If they want to watch it, it's there. We will cover it in the same way whether it's the first round of the FA Cup and we're at Accrington Stanley, or if it's the final of the FA Cup.

'The point is the gates have still gone up. People said at the beginning we couldn't show so many games because it would affect gates, but we were always of the opinion that if you show people how good the game is, if you make it high profile, you'll encourage kids to want to go. Sky has made a lot of players stars in the last three years. It's given ordinary players a much higher profile. The kids can associate with them more and more. They get their dads to take them to see these players. Grounds are being renovated and capacities falling, but attendances are actually rising and have been for three consecutive seasons while Sky have been covering games. And I think they will continue to do so.

'My role as co-commentator is to try to analyse what's happening. My boss has always told me, "Tell me something I don't know. I know that was a good pass, I know that was a goal, but why was that a good goal, why was that a bad mistake?" *The Bootroom* programme, with the arrows to illustrate moves and everything is an extension of that. People think it's easy but when you're doing everything else along the way, all the technical side of it, it can be quite demanding, but I enjoy it very much indeed.

'We had an awful lot of sceptics three years ago, far more than there were people behind us, but I think we've won over a lot of them because we don't rubbish the game. The people I work with, week in, week out, are all lovers of the game: the people in the studio, the people behind the scenes, and I think that comes through. Yes, I do get enthusiastic about things, but football is the most emotional sport in the world. No other sport has such a range of emotions and it's wonderful and I love to share them and I get involved in them and I think that's my job.

'I think my job's to keep the game simple. I've heard so much gobbledegook over 20 years when I was growing up, a lot of it coming across on the television screens, making things so complicated because it sounded nice. One of the things I try to do is keep it basically in working-class English. It's a working-class game and why complicate it? I try to keep it as simple as possible and easy to understand. The game's simplicity is without doubt the secret of its appeal worldwide.'

Watching football these days tends to be more comfortable for commentators as well as for supporters, but there are still reminders of the 'working-class game' for the men behind the mike.

'Most of the facilities at grounds have got better with the renovations,' Gray confirms, 'and most of the gantries are quite good. But in the early rounds of the FA Cup, when you don't know where you're going, you can bet your life that nine times out of ten the gantry is a piece of scaffolding that's had to be built for the occasion. One night about 18 months ago we did Port Vale against Stoke in the Cup and it absolutely threw it down. Ian Darke and I were on just such a piece of scaffolding, 70 feet in the air. There were 70mph winds, no cover and we were absolutely soaked to the skin. I've never had to commentate in conditions like it. All the technology was dripping, the monitors had gone, I had to gamble on when the slow-motions were on and we had one microphone, passing it to each other. It was farcical. But we got through the night and no-one would have known the problems we faced.

'But generally, now, the gantries are in keeping with grounds such as this,' he says, his eyes scanning the new Ewood Park. 'I obviously played at grounds that had the Holte Ends and the Stretford Ends and Kop ends, where people stood to watch their football, but I just think that when you look around now and see these magnificent stadiums, this is where football should be. It did take a tragedy for it to happen and I think football should have made its own decision to do this. But we can now go into the next century with a lot more confidence and belief in the game, more than we might have had with the older stadiums.'

Even the plushest of gantries cannot insulate the commentator from the most prevalent of occupational hazards, the goof.

'As you can imagine with me, there are millions of things that go wrong,' Gray cheerfully confesses. 'I mean, we've been on the road for three years and funny things do happen and you do say some daft things, but my favourite is when I cover Arsenal. There's the lad at Arsenal called Stefan Schwarz, and there's the motor cycle champion called Kevin Schwantz, and the number of times I have called Stefan Schwarz Kevin Schwantz on live television is unbelievable. But when you think it's 90 minutes, totally unscripted, and live, then what you say you are stuck with. So yes, we make lots of mistakes and my executive producer is quick to mention them at the end of games and we have a laugh and joke about them. But that's what makes it, the fact that it's not clinical and sometimes you do get things wrong.

'Having said that, I am full of admiration for the amount of work and preparation that Martin and Ian put into their jobs. They are both great to work with but different in many respects. The two days are different and you do treat them a little differently. Monday is a little more light-hearted. Martin is more intense about his commentary and Sundays tend to be a bit more serious.

'I think Martin's the best football commentator in the country and I'm pleased to say I was partly responsible for his signing. There were other commentators interested and they asked me for my opinion five years ago, and I said Martin. He was still a bit behind the Brian Moores and John Motsons then but I think he's gone on from there and is now the one who's setting the standards. And Sky are setting standards because we do have a different style of commentary. I come in when I like and it's basically two commentators working together – one, if you like, with journalistic knowledge, Martin or Ian, and one with footballing knowledge, me. It's very much an American type of commentary but one which, so far, I think the public enjoy.

'I feel we are getting through to people in the game, too, the clubs and managers. Obviously, managers are a little wary of television, especially when you're covering the run-ins to Championships and relegation and it can mean life or death at both ends of the table. I can understand it, having been in that situation. I know what it's like. People want to close ranks as they approach games and not allow us information, but I think most managers now know we are a bunch to be trusted. Anything we are told is in the strictest confidence. We try to get teams a little early so we can set up graphics and things, and managers are confident it doesn't go further than us until the right time. People at grounds are friendly to us and I think the fact that I played the game at the level I did helps. The players respect that in many ways.'

It is not just Gray, Tyler, Darke and Keys who turn up for Sky. There's an army of them.

'We have about 70 guys on the road,' Gray informs. 'This is another thing Sky don't get credit for. The BBC and ITV think it's a . . . well, it is, it's a huge job to put on live football, and they've had to do it maybe once a week, twice if they're pushing it. We do it twice as a norm. This week we will have covered Sunday, Monday, Wednesday, Thursday (the Youth Cup final) and then Sunday again, possibly two matches that day. So that will be five or six live games in one week. That's the crew that'll do that and it's a tremendous job to be able to do that, and at the standards the producers demand. They don't cut corners anywhere.'

So what is Gray's assessment of the season?

'I think on the pitch it has been a good season, an excellent season. There have been indiscretions, a major one obviously with Eric Cantona assaulting a fan, then we had Roy Keane stamping at the very time we were trying to talk about peace and had the managers on the pitch appealing for calm. But generally the football has been good and the four down has given us something we've never had before. Unfortunately, many managers have fallen by the wayside, more than half the 92. It's incredible.

'There's been the bungs, there's been the sleaze, there's been the allegations of match-rigging, there's been the drugs. That's unfortunate but I think we may have been guilty of having our heads in the sand if we believed a game that's paying young men as much money as it's paying them now was drug-free. It was always going to come out but it's how we react to it now that matters, how we make sure that as few players as possible fall into that drugs trap that is so easy to fall into. I know, as once a high profile youngster myself, that they attract an awful lot of the wrong people and with the money they're earning now they'll attract even more. I think if you quickly make examples, that's the key. If we continue to pussyfoot and do nothing then we'll continue to have problems. If the FA or whoever is responsible is seen to take swift and strong action then I think that's as good a deterrent as any to clean it up. I think the game's too big not to survive and go on.

'The one minus I think there has been from this season has been the problem we've had with referees. It's an old chestnut, particularly mine, but I do think this has been the poorest year I can remember in terms of the quality of referees. Their inconsistency has been unbelievable. I've watched games in Europe, in Scotland, in the English First Division, and I think the Premiership is the only league where referees have been trying to make the latest instructions work, and they haven't worked. I watched the Rangers versus Celtic game yesterday when tackles were flying in. There would have been one or two sent off, ten or 11 bookings in this country. The referee there just lets them get on with it, and why shouldn't he?

'What amazes me is that at the end of last season we all sat down and said what a fantastic season it had been. Supporters had enjoyed it all over the country, marvellous stuff, and we went and tried to change it. I find that incredible. The referees have not helped themselves, I don't think. You talk about wanting to protect the good players. Well, Ian Wright's on about 60 points; Peter Beardsley's been booked more times than he's ever been booked; Ryan Giggs has been booked. You know? I don't see how it has protected these players and I hope referees are going to take a look at themselves at the end of the season and say, "Wait a minute, we need to get together on this", because it hasn't worked at all.

'Referees now are just using the rules to suit themselves if decisions are made that are wrong. I'm not talking about giving penalties that aren't penalties and getting an offside wrong; that's touch and go because these things will always happen and we accept them. But I'm talking about Jason Wilcox being sent off at Nottingham Forest for dropping the ball on the touchline, a minute to go, and being sent off. I'm talking about things like that. That's not improving the game. I don't believe it for a minute. So that's been one of the downers for me and I just hope lessons are learned for next season.

'I just think the game is outstripping amateur referees, I really believe that now. The game is rushing ahead at such a pace. I've been banging the drum for professional referees for some 15 years now and I think we're heading that way. When you think of the experience that drops out of professional football every year, hundreds of players with 20 years' experience, not knowing what to do. Why not tap into that experience? Why not encourage them to become referees and linesman? The relationship between players and referees would be better and they would be answerable. At the moment they aren't. A referee can make a decision that might cost somebody, like that penalty decision Alan Wilkie made against Norwich at Leeds. I'm not saying that condemned Norwich to the First Division but it certainly contributed to it. Alan Wilkie can go home and go to his work and he's fine. He's not answerable to anyone, whether he makes bad decisions or good decisions.

'There's so much money in the game now and the FA have been paid so much they are going to have to start thinking about this. I was interested to hear Nigel Clough was going to take a refereeing course. He's got that experience of the game, he knows what's a bad tackle, he knows what's clumsy. He's been there. You won't see people like that throwing around yellow and red cards. We don't tap into it but we might in the next five or six years, you never know.'

Gray appears to tackle anything – playing, commentating and interviews – with equal zeal. He presumably knows no other way. He seems constantly airborne. Perhaps he inspired the naming of the channel. Somehow you don't imagine his coming to ground long enough to enjoy a break, a holiday.

'I know I have a great job, a job I love very much and I get time off in midweek, but it is a tough job and I do look forward to a good holiday. This week, for instance, I do Sunday, Monday, back home to the Midlands, then up to Manchester again on Wednesday to do United, then to London on Thursday to do *The Bootroom*, then back to wherever on Sunday for the deciders. I probably do 130 shows from August to May, which is a lot of television. I've probably commentated on 250 to 300 live games in three years. So we do get burnt out and thankfully Sky realise it's important to take time off in the summer to re-charge and get fresh for a new season.

'The main thing,' he adds with that familiar laugh, 'is to give the viewers a rest from my voice and my face.'

Blackburn won that night, United won on the Wednesday, so Sky had the final day drama they craved.

173

CHAPTER 19

Honest Day's Work

Roger Dilkes, referee

Come the end of any season, there is nothing left to be thrown at a Premiership referee. He has heard it all, seen it all. The criticism, the abuse, the theories and suggestions have been raining down on him throughout. He may be tired of the cynics and contemptuous of the detractors, but the chances are he will remain stoically philosophical, almost indifferent. Apparently the thick skin comes with the uniform.

But this past season, as Andy Gray's comments testify, the subject of refereeing has been even higher on the agenda; the man in the middle has been the man under the microscope as never before. Sometimes he has held up his hand and reversed a decision. Mostly he has not, even when subjected to the most intense pressure from players, managers, supporters and media.

Roger Dilkes is perhaps uniquely qualified to represent the referee in this very public debate. For most of the season he has officiated at Premiership matches, but for the last few weeks he has been forced to watch from the sidelines. Yes, referees get injured, too. He has viewed the game from every conceivable angle, considered every condemnation, pondered every prognosis. And he remains stoically philosophical.

In the real world Dilkes is a personnel manager with the Co-operative Wholesale Society. He lives in a neat but scarcely ostentatious brick, detached house at Mossley, in that South-East corner of Lancashire which creeps tentatively up the Pennines towards Yorkshire. Family pictures, particularly of his daughter, command wall space in the living room,though there is also a framed cartoon memento of the night he refereed Mark Hughes' testimonial match. The bearded Dilkes is confronted by the Manchester United striker executing his trademark scissors volley.

Gray will be interested to hear Dilkes is a former player. He was a semi-professional with Rochdale and played non-League football with Rossendale. The discipline of training has long been part of his life and he will be working on his fitness all summer, replenishing the wasted muscle, and be ready for the new campaign. At the age of 46, he is looking forward to two more seasons of refereeing.

As befits every sports person, he is in tracksuit bottoms and trainers and, as befits a referee, he delivers a precise update on his state of health.

'Basically, I've had both Achilles tendons sorted out. They've been giving me quite a bit of trouble from March time, so rather than continue I've been to hospital. Hopefully, I'll be fit for the new season.'

Rather unusually, for an ex-player, Dilkes preferred the option of refereeing to coaching.

'Initially I wanted to go on to the coaching side and I enjoyed the actual coaching, but I didn't enjoy being on the bench, watching at weekends. I felt I needed to get on to the field of play, hence taking up refereeing. So that was the route and fortunately for me I've come right the way through.'

Dilkes acknowledges the benefits a former player can bring to refereeing, yet also points out the flaws in Gray's argument.

'I think as a former player it does help me read the game, but it's not just about having played the game. There's an awful lot more to it than that, so I wouldn't subscribe to the theory that every former player could succeed as a referee. If a player is studying refereeing and refereeing matches midweek and coming through in exactly the same way as we've had to do while carrying out his playing profession, then that's right and proper, but you can't just switch from one to the other. I would suggest that's impossible. You need the grounding and experience of refereeing just as you need the grounding and experience of playing the game.'

And ...

'I honestly believe the old chestnut of professional referees wouldn't change the way we prepare and approach a game. To all intents and purposes we are virtually professional now. If people feel that referees going full-time professional would assist the game through their being fitter or more mentally attuned to the game and that they would give different sorts of decisions, that's all folly. It really is, because we train regularly now, we attend a series of conferences and training sessions throughout the year, both with our own association and in my case with the FA Premier League, and we watch videos, and we pull ourselves to pieces, constructively criticising situations we see. The fact that we'd be full-time employees of somebody like the FA wouldn't, I don't think, change matters at all.

'Currently a referee on the FA Premier League, which is all I can talk about, really, is paid £300 as a match fee. We receive expenses for travelling. If we have to stay overnight we have a hotel allowance and there's a meal allowance.

'To be honest, the subject of players' wages never crops up among referees. Good luck to them. We are all part of the same entertainment at the end of the day, but we don't compare our fees and conditions with the players'. We just go and do a job, and hopefully we do a good job.

'Certainly referees have been under the microscope this season, with the increased media coverage, particularly in the Premier League, where all games are televised. Every match is taped so you can't get away from it. I think a positive move, though, is having referees acting as the fourth official to colleagues in the Premier League. It is unfair to expect a linesman to come into the middle for an injured referee and equally for someone who's been refereeing, let's say, at Conference level, to then have to go and run the line. I've carried out the role of fourth official on a number of occasions.

'I would also say the English referees have carried out the FIFA mandatory instructions honestly throughout the season. We were advised by the Football Association that these were the mandatory instructions and we had to carry them out. We had training sessions and I honestly believe we have done that. It isn't the same in other parts of the world, as we've seen. All we can do in this country is continue as we've been told we should and it's for FIFA to get on to the other football associations in the other countries, and spell out and reinforce the mandatory instructions.

'I think in fairness, the Premier League clubs have accepted the new mandatory instructions. I think we've had better games from them, I think we've had more goals and I honestly believe that over a season we've not had as many injuries from tackles from behind, etc. So, overall in the season, and there'll always be highs and lows in everything, I think we've done very well. I think we've got it right and it's for others to catch up and do what we're doing.

'Whether a referee reverses a decision is up to the individual referee. If, through the Football Association, they've been asked to view a video on a contentious issue, then they themselves will have to make the decision on what they see. I think if a referee feels that a mistake has been made – and a number of them have changed their minds – then all credit to them. I think we are honest in all the decisions we make. We try hard to have a professional approach.

'Fortunately I haven't had any correspondence from the FA asking me to view a video, but I think I am my own critic when I view videos. I get a copy of every game I referee and watch them all. If I am critical of myself it's probably more to do with positioning. I say to myself, "Well, if you had been a bit wider or if you'd been a bit deeper you would probably have picked this up earlier or you might have seen that slightly differently and that might have been of advantage to the game."

'I've sent off one player this season, that was Don Hutchison, and I was quite happy with the decision. I think everyone was, because regrettably it was a bad tackle. Having been involved with the football fraternity a long time I don't think anybody likes to see players sent off, but having said that, they know where the lines are and if they cross them then they render themselves liable for disciplinary action.

'On occasions I think the microscopic look at us has been a bit too severe. I think some of the incidents, had we not had live television, probably wouldn't have even had a mention in the papers. But probably that game has gone on without an incident, then the media have tried to look for things. When you consider there are 20-odd cameras at games now, the chances are they'll find something.

'I certainly don't think we should have a touchline referee. If you look at cricket now, with their umpire in the stand, he's only giving decisions on run-outs or stumpings, or the player not getting into the crease. The other thing is that cricket is played over a considerable number of hours, even days. Football is all about movement and momentum and thrills and spills, and I don't think on a cold afternoon in the middle of winter that the crowd would thank you for saying, "Well, hang on a minute, we'll just have a look if that ball was out of play, or if did it go in the goal, or was it a free-kick, or whatever." If that ever came into the game I believe we'd lose some of the enjoyment. I certainly wouldn't subscribe to the use of technology by an official in the stand. I don't think it would work.'

Dilkes is also usually spared the critical eye of his family in the stand.

'My wife and daughter come to only the odd game, but in the main I travel with a colleague who's good company for me on the long drives. They stay at home. They've got their own interests. But they do watch me on television and pull my leg a bit. There's always some good-humoured banter in the house and that's good.'

It is not so good if the inevitable criticism of referees penetrates the sanctuary of the household.

Dilkes says: 'I've been lucky over the years in that I've not had any serious criticism that has affected my family. You will always have the odd, isolated incident, which I tend to just forget about. I think my shoulders are broad enough and I've been around long enough to be able to do that. You get the odd call, the odd letter, but I suppose in the top flight you need to be lucky when you referee and I've probably had a little bit of luck which others might not have had.

'You hear on the grapevine about your colleagues getting stick and various things and we can obviously report any such incidents to the FA. But I think the attitude of referees is that they prefer just to get on with the next game and after a couple of weeks it's gone. Time is a great healer.'

Like Neil Midgley and many referees, Dilkes is a talker.

'It's always been part of my game, whether playing or refereeing, because I believe if you can communicate with a player and get on to the same wavelength it can be a considerable benefit. Neil is a top class referee and has been very good to me personally over the years. He's taught me an awful lot. I'm a different type of person to Neil but like him I feel it's got to be good to communicate with the players because if you can do that and they understand that you're in control then they can enjoy their game.

'I don't think players get branded by referees. I've had a lot of contact with so-called problem players and never had a problem with them. I don't believe for one minute that referees go out on a park and say, "I'm refereeing such-and-such a game today and this team has three players who are bad lads and I'm going to make sure they don't step out of line." It just doesn't happen. We take each game as it comes.

'So-called moaning players can be misunderstood, too. A lot of the time, believe it or not, it's nervous tension on their part. And whilst they're talking a lot, they're not doing anything wrong. They're not showing dissent, they're not having a go. Paul Ince is a fair example. I've never refereed him because he's too close to where I live, but there are other players who are exactly the same as Paul Ince, who do a lot of talking. They are motivating their own players a lot of the time and they need that to lift them.'

If no referee should hold terror for a player, then no ground or team should hold terror for a referee, according to Dilkes.

'I've no qualms about going to any ground in the country, Premier or Endsleigh League. FA Cup appointments could take us to any ground. I think referees always have their favourite grounds, though. I like going to Aston Villa. I refereed my first First Division game there. I did Villa-Luton Town. Many years ago. The crowd there get behind their side. Maybe not so much this season because they've not been so successful, but in the main they are very vociferous, they can lift it, and a referee can respond to that just as a player does.

'I like going to all the grounds in the North-East. That's a real hot-bed of football, and it doesn't matter whether it's your Darlingtons, your Hartlepools or whether it's at St James' or Roker or Middlesbrough, I could do one of those every week of the year. I enjoy talking with people about football because I am basically a football fan too, and they're all football people in the North-East.

'A team I would referee any time is Nottingham Forest and I say that without hesitation because the players there, previously under Mr Clough [*note the respectful address*] and now under Frank Clark, have had just the same discipline, and have played the same lovely football. More often than not they play it on the floor. It doesn't matter what side they're playing, you can guarantee you're going to get a good game of football. The game at Hillsborough, when they got seven, must have been a joy to watch.

'I suppose this season I've had some difficult games – derby games, FA Cup appointments, Coca Cola Cup games – but because they are hard they can be all the more enjoyable and satisfying when you come out of them feeling you've done all right. I did the

Ipswich-Norwich game early in the season, which was a live game, and I was also fortunate enough to referee the Blackburn-Liverpool Coca Cola Cup game – both very, very good games, but highly charged and at the end of the 90 minutes you come away feeling good about it.

'You can appreciate the commitment and quality of the play. Ian Rush scored a hat-trick in the match at Blackburn but early on they could have lost it. It was backs to the wall. Liverpool had to take an awful lot of pressure but then started to dominate, particularly in midfield, and I thought on the night Michael Thomas played exceptionally well considering he'd just come back from a long spell injured. Rush, though, was just out of this world. It was a pleasure to see that hat-trick from close angles. Brilliant.'

Just as vivid are the not so satisfying performances.

'I think if I'm honest I would have to recall a game I had a couple of seasons ago down at Peterborough. I just wasn't happy with my performance at all on that day. I didn't particularly get a bad Press and the crowd will always give you stick. You can have a blinder and still get stick, but that's just life. If you give a decision you're right for one and wrong for the other. At that particular game I just didn't feel afterwards, when I analysed what we'd done that day, that my colleagues and I had done it as well as we should have done. I think you've got to be honest enough to say that.

'Fortunately, I can look back on a lot of games for the right reasons. Some will say Wembley appointments and things like that are the highlights of careers, and I suppose that's right. I've been lucky enough to do Wembley games. I've refereed the FA Trophy final and last season I did one of the FA Cup semi-finals there. But an awful lot of the derby games I've done are the ones that come to mind. Again, it comes back to the passion of the players, the passion of the crowds, and you've really got to work hard to keep control.

'I've refereed Everton-Liverpool, I've refereed a considerable number of London derbies, all the North-East derbies, some in the Midlands and, as I've said, the East Anglian one. I wouldn't get the Manchester one because of where I live but that's all right. I get to all the other parts of the country and it gives the other lads a chance to come to Manchester.'

180

Nothing eases the tension of a match more swiftly or effectively than a shaft of humour and Dilkes has inevitable 'take-outs' to relate.

'One of the funniest things that happened to me was at Burnley, when I was a linesman, and I was supervising a corner. The lad put the ball down, went to kick it as I moved round on to the goal-line, and instead of kicking the ball kicked the flag. The flag just took off and it was like a dart travelling towards me and players standing ten yards from the corner. We all had to take evasive action.

'As I've mentioned, you get a lot of talking on the field and in many instances players do help referees. You can have a word with someone and say, "Look, just have a word with such-and-such-a-body", and they can help you out. I'll always remember refereeing Leeds once when Vinny Jones was there and Gordon Strachan was captain. Gordon's quite a vociferous character, one of those who gets himself pumped up by talking. I'd really had enough of him and I said to Vinny Jones, "Vinny, will you tell Gordon Strachan to shut up", and he turned round and said to Gordon, in his own style, "Gordon, belt up, I'm even getting a bloody headache!" In a nice way, that quietened Gordon down and we got on with the game.

'Again, communicating with players, and I think that's what it's all about. That goes unrealised. Some people might see me talking to a player and think I'm warning him, but in many instances I'm saying, "That was a good pass", or "Good shot", or "Unlucky, son", or whatever. Sometimes, later in the game, that may go for you. If you're having a bit of a problem they may come in and help you out. Quid pro quo. That's what it's all about.'

What players and referees do have in common is superstitions, those little routines and idiosyncrasies without which their entire world would cave in. Some like to change early, some late; some must put on their right boot first, or their left; some like to be last on the pitch; some like to finish changing on the pitch; some like their shirt out and socks down, even when they are not supposed to; many now wear their collars up.

'There are probably two or three things I make sure of,' Dilkes confides. 'I always lace my boots at the ground. I always take my rings off. That's a superstition but now I think it's important because we in fact ask players to take their rings off for safety reasons.

We have a bell to tell the players when we want them to go out and I always like to press that three times. I just do. And the other thing is that I always like to turn the light off in the dressing-room before we come out. I like to be in control from start to finish and I think when we're going out on the field of play, if I switch the light off then I know the lads are with me and we're there as a team. It's something I've always done. It's probably psychological.'

But is it really worth it?

'Why do I referee? Yes, we're always asked. I think football is in my blood. My father used to say if there were GCE's for football then I'd have had a dozen. I've been involved in football since I played for my home town team, Hyde, as a ten-year-old. The lads I played with then and myself have had a great time out of football for 30-odd years and we're still having a great time out of football. That's why I do it, just to be involved in football.'

Tomorrow is FA Cup final day, Everton versus Manchester United, and the focus of Dilkes' attention will not be in blue or red, but in black.

'I'll definitely be watching it from Gerald Ashby's point of view. I find it very difficult now to watch a football game from a spectator's point of view. Very often when I'm watching a game now, even before the commentator has said a particular thing it's already gone through my mind. I'll be running every step with Gerald. He'll be nervous – he'll need that to get the adrenalin flowing – but he's an excellent referee.

'It's a big occasion for the players and the supporters, but it's also a big occasion for Gerald Ashby. It's his highlight. He's a FIFA referee, he's refereed all over the world, and now it's tremendous for him to get his final. He'll enjoy it and so will his colleagues, who are with him. I just hope the ball runs kindly for him, there are no contentious issues and it's a good game. Tomorrow night when he's having his meal, if that's what's happened, he'll be well pleased.'

CHAPTER 20

Family Affair – Part One

Chesterfield Supporters' Club

It was 2–0. Against Derby. Third Division North. Horrifying to realise it was also the 1955–56 season. But then when you are born no more than a bent free-kick – or a Crooked Spire – from the ground it is only natural you should be plucked straight from the cradle and deposited on to the terraces at Saltergate.

Almost 40 years on from that first match at Chesterfield – that first match anywhere – it is an appropriate time to retrace the original steps into the dream-land exclusive to football folk. A win for Chesterfield tonight, against Mansfield, will take them to Wembley for the Third Division play-off final against Bury or Preston. The Spireites came away from Field Mill with a 1–1 draw and, in front of an 8,000-plus sell-out crowd, are favourites to go through.

Morally they should, anyway. They were only just beaten to an automatic promotion place by Walsall. But since when did morality, fairness or justice have anything to do with it? The play-off system brings in more money and prolongs the drama, but it also piles on the agony and makes you want to quit in despair if you are beaten by a team that finished below you in the table. Well, at least until next season, that is.

The first sign of any ground approaching is the dreaded row of cones. Bet there was none here in 1955–56. There again, who drove to football matches in 1955–56? Round the corner from the ground's main entrance, the social club is already a-buzz. Bet that wasn't here in 1955–56, either. Brian, a wiry-looking figure, greets the regulars in the time-honoured way they do round here: 'm' duck'. Male or female, any age, it's 'm' duck'.

A self-proclaimed lifelong supporter ambles from the bar to the reception area, pint clamped in hand, and asks if anyone has a spare ticket or knows where he might get one. He's got a tenner, he says, for a ticket. He explains he was working away last week and got home at the weekend to discover all the tickets had been sold. He's got a tenner for a ticket. He doesn't normally miss a match. Follows them through thick and thin. He's got a tenner for a ticket. He's still got the stub from a match in the 'Thirties, when his grandad took his dad. Record crowd. According to the official club information, the record attendance is 30,968, versus Newcastle United, Division Two, 7 April 1939. Could have sworn he said Spurs, 1934, or was it 34,000? Anyway, he's got a tenner for a ticket.

In both bars, members of the Supporters' Club, their tickets tucked safely in their pockets and bags, are into the pre-match ritual enacted across the land. Drink and comment flow in roughly equal amounts. Among some anticipation is high, among others trepidation is acute. You often find the most earnest fans are also the most pessimistic, and tonight they are nervous. And even if they get to Wembley, would it be another let-down. Remember last time? (1990, beaten 1–0 by Cambridge, scorer: Dion Dublin. Those strands!)

This is no executive suite, centenary room or jubilee lounge, just a social club, full of the working-class people of Andy Gray's working-class game. There are men and women of all ages, the strong and the infirm, a perfect representation of a real football following. Chesterfield's rare brush with national fame is the fans' brush with something a little special, too. But then their devotion is guaranteed regardless. They will stick together as families do and, as we shall hear, many of them regard their Supporters' Club as a family. The sense of belonging, to the game and especially to a team, can be that strong. That important.

Football is just about everything to Paul Brownlow, and a blessing to his mother. Paul is 35 and wheelchair-bound, condemned to disability from birth by spina bifida. He has supported Chesterfield for 21 years. He can recall without hesitation that his love affair started in the 1974–75 season. His mother, Mary Smith, took on the responsibility of bringing Paul to the matches after the death of her second husband. She drives him from their home at Barlborough, just outside Chesterfield, to Saltergate but they travel on the Supporters' Club bus to away games.

'I've always watched football,' says 54-year-old Mary, refuting the theory that the female football fan is a modern phenomenon. 'We used to follow Barlborough for a good many years, local football, you know. My other lad, Carl, was only little then. He would have been about three and Paul ten when we followed Barlborough. Carl's not as interested in football now, though.'

Paul: 'He's not disabled. I've tried to get him interested but he's not bothered. He'll watch football on television, but that's about it. He's not really a football man, like me. I was always interested. I've been in a wheelchair all my life so I was never able to play football with all the other kids. I would have played and pushed and tried to be good. I like most sports. Not gymnastics or swimming or anything like that. It's boring. I don't like badminton, either. I'm mad keen on horse-racing. I'm not an expert, but I'm mad keen on it. And cricket, especially the limited overs cricket. I go to college two days a week to do computers and I do pottery. But football and Chesterfield are my main love. Got to be.'

Mary: 'It was broken for a while, though, when my husband died. Paul kept on about wanting to go again but I'd only just learned to drive and I didn't like coming into town for a bit. Well, when they got Liverpool in the Cup I made an effort. It was a beauty of a match and we gave them a good run for it. And we've been coming ever since. I'm as wild about Chesterfield as he is now.'

Paul: 'My other team is Liverpool, actually, but we all have a second team. My number one team is Chesterfield. I believe in supporting the place I come from rather than supporting anybody bigger. It's easy to support big teams. I come to the reserves, also, midweek afternoons. They're a very good side, also.'

Mary: 'We come to all the home matches ...'

Paul: 'And a lot of the away matches as well.'

Mary: 'I bring him to home matches. He's strong, he lifts himself in, I don't have to lift him. We travel away on the Supporters' Club coach and they're very good. They lift him on and off, the lads do, for me. We don't have many problems now at grounds. Chesterfield were a bit awkward at one time but things are a lot better now. I pay for the coach but mostly, in this division, they let us in free. There's not many charge. Chesterfield don't.

And those that do charge only for me, about £5. I go into the enclosure here with Paul and sit alongside him.

'I just wish some clubs would think more about where they put us. Sometimes you can't see for the barriers. We're nearly always away from the other fans inside the grounds.'

Paul: 'Some of the clubs have got bad views, but not many of them. There was a silly ramp at Mansfield that I didn't like. They help me down but I still don't like it. It's quite steep. But it's a good view when you get there. It's money that's the problem at some grounds, at small clubs.

'I went to Wembley in '90 and the only criticism I've got there is that there's only wheelchair space at one end and I like to go with my own supporters at any game. I wouldn't mind segregation into my own little crowd, or "family" as I prefer to put it. The fans who travel with us are good friends. Always helpful.'

Mary: 'It is like a family. It's nice travelling together. My friend here, she's been footballing since she was a ten-year-old and she's 80 next. [*Modern phenomenon indeed!*] She's got a rabbit's foot with her for luck.'

The friend. Gwen Blockley, chips in: 'I take it to the bingo, as well.'

Mary: 'And we keep us fingers crossed all through t' match.'

Gwen: 'There were two fellas in here about a fortnight ago, and I says, "Do you know what's a matter with them?" They said, "No". I said, "The ball, they want a brick in it. It's too light. It keeps going over t' bar. Not like the old ones".'

This woman's talk is all very well but Paul has some serious points to make: 'We want to go to Wembley this time and win the thing. That's the priority now. I'll go again if they get through, without doubt. Even if I have to push my wheelchair all the way there, I'll be there. If that's what it takes I'll do it, on my own. Let's have all Derbyshire down there.

'The team has done well to do what it's done, even if we end up getting nothing at the end of tonight. We've done what we could. We got off to a bad start, halfway through the season we were approximately tenth, and to get this close to promotion we've done extremely well. Let's just hope we can see the job through. John Duncan is an excellent manager. He's brought us this close and no matter what the cynics may say, if we fail now it will be a case of hard lines, not throwing it away.

'I suppose I think like a manager when I'm at a game. I like total quietness. I want to go into a deep trance and don't want anybody bothering me, saying the wrong thing. I just want to sit there. As far as I'm concerned I'm t' gaffer. I let my emotions out when I'm watching a match, though, as much as I can. It could get emotional tonight.

'It's not likely to be very friendly, not on local derby day and with so much at stake. I would say it's going to be blood and guts. We know our own supporters and it's a nice atmosphere. It's like a family. It is a family, in fact. But tonight it's us versus them. We love our lot, we hate them lot. The result is the thing tonight. As long as John Duncan gets round the boys and we give our all, we can do it. Let's do it.'

Rival fans are not known for their sensitivity and Paul is conscious he could be a soft target for the more barbaric who attach themselves to football.

'It depends how ardent fans they are and what state of mind they are in that afternoon or evening,' he says. 'I don't tend to get personal insults too much, but I have heard it on the ground. How hard it is to take depends on who it's aimed at. If it's not aimed at me I don't mind so much, but it's not very nice to hear it, of course it's not. It shouldn't be said but you're always going to get it, unfortunately.'

Paul is wearing, for this tribal battle, a blue and white Chesterfield cap and, beneath his jacket, a blue and white Chesterfield first choice shirt. 'When I go to away games I wear the green and white stripes [*the change strip*] irrespective of whether they are playing in green and white or blue and white on the day. I change every time away.'

The away strip is part of the new culture. So is the fanzine. Paul is into that, too.

'I don't believe we are always told the truth about our club,' he declares, provocatively. 'I prefer to buy the fanzine, where the supporter has the top say. They are the top dogs. The supporters are the paying public. They have their say and, at the end of the day, what they say I believe. I buy the programme, for the facts and figures of the club – first team, reserves, juniors. I'm into that kind of thing, as long as we are told the truth. I believe the home truths are in the fanzine.'

Mary smiles a mother's smile. You can only wonder how she has coped with her ordeal these past 35 years. Football, for all its faults and failings, has at least served to lighten the load a little.

'Football is a release for me,' she says, 'because it has been hard, especially since my husband died. I had to learn to drive when I could see he was getting tired. I pulled a trailer to go on holiday but not for the last three years. I think I've lost my bottle a bit. At first I made myself go. We'd go looking for bowling greens, sit around and watch. I used to take my knitting. I take him cricketing sometimes in summer but I'm not stuck on it. I find it's a bit boring but he likes it.'

Gwen manoeuvres her stick so she can lean over to say: 'She's a wonderful mother. She's had him like that since he was born. And she's never let him go anywhere. She's just stuck to him. And if anyone deserves a Heart of Gold she does. Think about 30-odd years. It's a long time. She'll get her reward somewhere, I'm sure of that.'

Right now Mary will settle for Wembley and then the Second Division. 'Oh, yes, I'm looking forward to Wembley. Gwen's already booked the coach. And I think they can win down there this time, too. Besides, we want them to go up so we can go to some different grounds, don't we, Gwen?'

An hour before kick-off, as Mary pushes Paul through the door, the social club is heaving. In the other room, Supporters' Club secretary, Roy Frisby – appropriately named since he seems forever flying from one matter of urgency to another – pauses briefly mid-air to talk about Paul, Mary and his organisation.

'At the Supporters' Club we just feel it's right to look after them because they wouldn't get to the match otherwise. Mary couldn't manage Paul on her own to away matches, so the lads are happy to lift him in and off the coach. We have quite a few coaches but make sure we have somebody to look after them. Paul enjoys travelling on the coach with the fans. He's always got plenty of banter and joins in the chat. I think he knows the way to every ground now.

'There's a disabled enclosure inside the football club and people arrange for tickets. Disabled spectators don't pay to go in, which is good PR. You find that at nearly all the home matches the enclosure is full. Some of the away grounds don't seem to be so well organised. At Fulham Paul had to sit on the away end, which didn't seem quite right, but usually the disabled are looked after.

'Mary's amazing, really. A lot of people wouldn't bring Paul. They wouldn't take the risk. I hope she still comes with him next year, when we are hopefully going to be in a higher division.'

The Supporters' Club have set up shop with their paraphernalia on the stage at the far end of the room and Donna Siddon, a committee member, reports brisk business.

'I try to get to every game I can but I'm a nurse so it's difficult,' she says. 'I'm only coming to half a game tonight. I'm on nights. But I wanted to be here for at least part of it.'

Husband Chris is also helping out. Like Paul, he wants to give John Duncan credit for getting Chesterfield this far. 'The secret is shrewd management,' he says. 'I think the addition of Phil Robinson and Tony Lormor has made a difference.'

Success has also meant additional supporters wanting to jump on the bandwagon. 'Suddenly we've found we've got a lot more fans. You notice that when you're manning the shop and they come for programmes not realising the price has gone up from £1 to £1.20. You see people coming with Sheffield Wednesday shirts but hopefully we can stop them going to Hillsborough and get them to come to Saltergate more often. We are Chesterfield through and through. I've never been to support another team.'

Donna: 'It's easy to say you support a big team. You see them all walking round town with different shirts on.' (There was further, disturbing evidence of this on the drive into town: a youth wearing a Blackburn shirt. In Chesterfield!)

Chris: 'It's quite easy to support success. If you go to a lot of these people who wear Man United shirts and say, "Have you ever been to Old Trafford?", they'll most likely say, "No." They're armchair supporters. But people in here are true Chesterfield supporters.'

The plight of disabled Chesterfield supporters is a subject close to his heart.

'I actually work for the Health Authority Disability Services. They are on about building a new ground here and facilities for the disabled is one of the things that wants looking at. I think they must feel away from the crowd where they watch from here. Access and viewing positions are better at the newer grounds.

'At Lincoln, for instance, the disabled are in with the rest of the crowd and I think that's a lot better. They stand out when they are on their own and I don't think that's right. At Northampton now there's a space every so often for a wheelchair, not spaces in just one area. They are dotted around the ground. I've only been doing this job about seven months but it's amazing when you are doing a job like this that you notice how many people are in wheelchairs and what the facilities for them are like.

'Paul is passionate about his football and it's important he and others like him can get to matches in reasonable comfort and also that they feel part of the crowd. They just want to be regarded as supporters. I know Paul's worried about tonight but hopefully we'll do it and be off down to Wembley.'

But will Donna be able to make it?

'Oh, yes, definitely,' she says. 'I'll not miss that. I put a request in for that day off a long time ago.'

Paul is among some 15 supporters in the disabled enclosure, beneath the stand. Fans still stand on the other three sides of Saltergate. The Mansfield end is behind the goal to the right. You'll find not only terracing here, but that associated tradition long lost to the age of the all-seater stadia: the home fans moving from behind the goal their team are attacking in the first half to an area as close as possible to the other end for the second half.

It is a fraught evening for all Chesterfield supporters. Twice down, they also have their goalkeeper, Andy Beasley, carried off injured. It is not a good omen. The goalkeeper is something of a sacred cow in this town. Chesterfield is as famous for its goalkeepers as its Crooked Spire. This misfortune, however, is more than compensated for by the dismissal of two Mansfield players and eventually Chesterfield's power-and-pressure game proves irresistible. They win 5–2 after extra time, 6–3 on aggregate.

And so to Wembley and the play-off final against Bury. Goals in the first half by Lormor and Robinson, and obdurate resistance in the second ensured victory and promotion for Chesterfield. It was 2–0.

190

CHAPTER 21

Family Affair – Part Two

Graham Turner, manager, and his wife, Ann

English football has taken an even heavier toll on its managers this past year, swelling the ranks of the unemployed and heightening the tension among those still in work. No matter how many times the carousel stops, there is no guarantee of another ride. Some give up and walk away to a new job, a new life. Others continue to wait in hope, and in faith.

Graham Turner has waited in hope and faith since he parted company with Wolverhampton Wanderers in March 1994. Comforted by the cushion of a further season on his contract, he took the opportunity to enjoy a break from the pressures and tribulations of management. The holidays and fishing trips served to recharge the batteries, but catching work was not so easy. He was competing not only with other experienced managers, but also with the constant flow of burgeoning hopefuls.

Turner committed himself to this dubious craft at homely Shrewsbury Town, initially as player-coach, then player-manager. He led them from the Third Division to the Second and seemingly endless, heroic Cup conquests. A big job was inevitable. It materialised at Aston Villa. Trophies, however, did not and he had to come to terms with dismissal. So, too, did his family: his wife, Ann, and their four children, Neil, Mark, Samantha and Andrew.

They were to find a new cause and a new home, ramshackle though it was, at Molineux. The empire that was Wolves had been in spectacular decline. They were now, in 1986, in the Fourth Division. But this, Turner sensed, was the perfect time to move in. Surely, he felt, a club so rich in tradition and potential, could go only one way from here. And what a thrill and privilege it would be to resurrect the club he revered as a boy.

The revival was as dramatic as he dared envisage. Promotion eluded Wolves that first spring but not the next, nor the one after that. They were champions in consecutive seasons. The signing of Steve Bull, who cost £60,000 from West Bromwich Albion, proved an inspired piece of business. His classic centre-forward play, his hunger and his amazing bombardment of goals symbolised Wolves' ascent. A levelling off was not so amazing, especially when the club had to give priority to the rebuilding of the ground, yet the natives, and the new chiefs, grew restless and, despite having taken Wolves to the sixth round of the FA Cup and the fringe of the promotion contest in 1994, Turner accepted it was time to close this chapter in his career.

Once again, the family had had to share the ordeal; the misery and the abuse. These are not burdens that can be left on the doorstep. Ann and the children had all been regulars at matches. Mark was even a player with the club. He was to move to Northampton and the rest of the family were fully prepared to leave their home at Little Aston, near Sutton Coldfield, and begin a new life. More than once they were encouraged to check out housing and schools, only to be disappointed. They even considered going abroad.

Turner is not without friends in the game and was given scouting missions by Derby County. He served on transfer tribunals and welcomed occasional local radio stints. All of which enabled him to stay in touch and retain some profile in the game. But into June 1995, he was still an unemployed manager.

Ann Turner admits she has enjoyed the past year, but her husband is at pains to stress he is itchy for work. 'I've enjoyed the rest, I've enjoyed the time off, yeah, because I've had plenty to do, but I want to get back into it. When I left Wolves I never thought for a minute I would still be without a job 15 months later. That's partly my own fault. I turned down one or two, didn't feel they suited me, and missed out. I hit the post with Ipswich and one or two other jobs. I looked abroad and either didn't fancy it or the timing was wrong.

'But the 15 months has absolutely flown by. We've had some fun, there's no doubt about that. I've played golf, enjoyed salmon and trout finishing and we've had plenty of holidays. It's been, in some ways, pleasant waking up, particularly on a Saturday morning, without the problems you face normally as a manager, because there's no doubt about it, whatever people say, there is a lot of pressure involved in it and most of it is self-imposed. It's not financial pressure or anything of that nature, it's just wanting to be successful, and I think I've enjoyed the break from that pressure.

'Then, as the weeks go by, you want to get back into it. You want to get involved in the day-to-day training and everything. I was one who was always out on the training ground, never enjoyed being in the office, never enjoyed driving down motorways, but that was part and parcel of it. You had to go and watch matches. But the enjoyment was being on the training ground.

'There is a financial pressure on me now and that does come into it. In the early months you think you'll be very selective. Something doesn't appeal to you so you knock it on the head. It comes to the stage where you can't afford to be so selective.'

Ann, too, has relished the release from match-day traumas.

'I don't think you realise what a different person you can be until you have that break from it. You are a different person in as much as you can enjoy normal things in life like going on a shopping trip, or spontaneous laughter on a Saturday morning. I think it's our fault, as a family. We've made him bring it home. We've shared everything there. It would be so easy to let him go out and say it's a job of work and not think about it; spend the money and just enjoy yourself. But that wouldn't be fair on Graham. You've got to be there.'

Graham attempts to lighten the mood: 'That's the problem of finding a new club now because the first thing we have to make sure of is that we get five seats in the directors' box. You need a big directors' box for the Turner family. In fairness, going back to the Shrewsbury days and right through, they've always come, not only to home matches but all over the country as well. So it has been that thing where the family have got involved.'

Ann: 'Graham lost the Villa job just before Neil's birthday and he was devastated, the whole family were. It spoilt the birthday. Doing the job that Graham does the kids have been very supportive and at Aston Villa, because they were in a Birmingham school, they took an awful lot of stick and criticism. Defending their father at school is an everyday factor for a football manager's children. I mean, it's Graham's job and it's up to me to accept the things that come with it, but for the children it is very, very difficult.

'At one point one of them used to sit on the windowsill in the house thinking it was a lucky place to sit on a Saturday afternoon because one day they were sitting there and the team happened to win. It shouldn't be like that and you try to take them out of it, but I used to be superstitious and go through the ritual of what colours to wear, all that sort of thing. Then I realised killing magpies and burying them didn't really work! I'm sure we had magpies who knew what we were thinking and used to make a point of hanging from the guttering upside down and making sure we could see only one head of a magpie.'

Graham: 'I think it's particularly hard for Ann and the kids. There was one particular incident at half-time at Villa, when Ann was spat on by some of the crowd behind the directors' box.

'I don't think the Villa parting was any harder than at Wolves. It doesn't get any easier. But I would have liked a little bit longer at Villa. I'd done two years, two months and I made sure the bulk of the money had gone into young players, and they were coming on, but at that level patience is in very short supply. I left Dorigo, Elliott, Keown, Hodge, Daley and Walters, all young players who went on to be internationals or go on for big money. I'd concentrated on forming what I considered was a nucleus of a good side.

'I'm not sure that I tried to do a little too much too quickly, as has been suggested. The European Cup-winning side was still breaking up, people like Withe, Mortimer, Bremner, Evans were coming to the end of their careers, hadn't really been replaced and all that had to be sorted out. But it was a while before we made major changes and I kept all the existing staff on to ensure some continuity and not make changes for the sake of it.

'I won't allow myself to be bitter about the Wolves situation but it is hard to take when you look back to what was achieved there, pulling the club round, gates going up from 2,500 to 23,000, new ground and everything else. We'd won two Championships, we'd been to Wembley and got nearly £1 million in the bank before the Haywards came in with their big money. So most of the success was achieved on a shoestring.

'I don't think many clubs could have been as low as Wolves was when we went in there – the place itself, the ground, the position of the club, three successive relegations, two receiverships, nearly out of business again. People see the nice ground and tend to forget that. There were rats running around the corridors – and I'm not just referring to some of the players! You wouldn't have given the balls to a Sunday league side. They'd had no new kit for three years. Tommy Docherty had been there and taken Wolves into his music hall act. They were the butt of everybody's jokes, not only in the Midlands but through football in general. All that was turned around.

'When the Haywards came in the big money at first was spent on the ground and in fairness the last summer I had there I was given £3 million to spend, which I put into Geoff Thomas, David Kelly, Kevin Keen and Peter Shirtliff. Thomas was a real driving force and took some persuading to come, but unfortunately we lost him fairly early on through injury and then Bully, too. We failed to get promotion and you have got to pay the penalty. It was entirely my decision.

'Having reached the quarter-finals of the FA Cup and lost at Chelsea, we went to Portsmouth two days later, and although there wasn't much time to do anything with the team after the Cup disappointment, I felt that if it went wrong at Portsmouth it would be the right time to resign. After seven-and-a-half years and a lot of success the crowd had turned considerably against me. It was hard to bear but it was understandable because people have short memories and are impatient. I always thought I would see it through because it had been my club from being a kid. I knew how much work had been put into it.'

It is common knowledge in the Midlands that the chairman, Jonathan Hayward, son of the club's benefactor and president, Sir Jack Hayward, vented his frustration on the team coach after the match at Portsmouth, but Turner plays down the significance of the incident.

'What happened on the coach is immaterial,' he insists. 'I'd already decided before then. The chairman had a little go at the players, the first time I'd ever known it, but that's Jonathan. I think he was new to the game, perhaps a little naive and didn't realise fully what was going on, how hard it was for the players to come back just two days after losing the quarter-final. There were still 13 games to go, I'd enjoyed my time there and I thought if they got a new manager in quickly there was still time for them to make the play-offs.

'Most of the players I left have still been in the side this season and I would have liked to see them get promotion. People like Steve Bull. Twenty-nine games he's played this season and got 19 goals. He's got to be my best signing – £40,000 initially and £20,000 more after games. Two minutes in the boardroom it took to get him. We offered him £225 a week in the Fourth Division and he has never been an ounce of trouble for the club. We were worried when he went to Italy with the England World Cup squad, thinking he'd come back with big ideas and wanting to leave, but no. I had a super relationship with him.

'I have felt since I left Wolves there is a danger you can stay at a club too long. Three or four years ago Ron Atkinson said to me – and I will always remember his words – "Your stock is high in the game at the moment, don't stay at Wolves too long." Nick Faldo referred recently to a "comfort zone" and in management you build up a club, your position becomes seemingly impregnable and things start to slip away. You maybe lose that bit of drive that a fresh challenge would induce. I've looked at some managers this season, managers of big clubs, and wondered whether they haven't just lost that edge they had a year or two ago. With hindsight, there's not a shadow of a doubt I was at Wolves two-and-a-half years too long. If I'd gone then, people would have been knocking on the door. Instead I'm looking for a job!

Ann: 'As far as the family was concerned, leaving Wolves was heart-breaking because the children had grown up there. It was a family club when we first went there – usually just one family, us. We went to the games and for seven-and-a-half years we lived with it, all of us, Sam included. The kids grew up there and we were part of the club. We were very, very proud of it, and from going to school and having the others mocking them – "Wolverhampton Wanderers? You must be kidding!" – it became pats on the back and "Well done, you're going to the Premier". We didn't want him to leave it there. We all pleaded with him not to resign. We still felt he could have got to the Premier last year.'

Graham has looked on, this past season, while other managers have suffered, stumbled and fallen.

'The ones you feel for are the likes of Brian Horton, at Manchester City. He'd been sacked in the Press every week for months and months. I've looked at him in television interviews, black rings round his eyes, and it's not the Brian Horton I knew. He looked in need of a rest. He won't agree, but leaving City might be a blessing for him. The pressure didn't seem to come from people within the club or the team. He bought some good players. I think

Rosler's a terrific signing. So I sympathise with him because the axe hung over him for so long and that's the hard part to live with, and it can't have helped being in a city where United have once again been dominating.'

Turner's biggest personal disappointment this past season has been missing out on the Ipswich Town job.

'They were still in the Premiership and I've always thought it to be a good club, a stable club. The set-up is superb there; the training ground, gymnasium. And it's a nice place to take your family to live. I would have fancied the challenge there.'

Ann: 'I'm quite happy to move, particularly to a place like Ipswich. I don't think you can turn your nose up at anywhere. Losing the Ipswich job after being so close did affect me because we have nice memories of the club – we used to play them regularly in the FA Cup and do well, so it would have been a nice twist in the tail if Graham had ended up being manager there, a nice story. The vibes were so good. One reporter was phoning constantly from Ipswich, saying Graham was very popular and looking good for the job. Now when jobs come up the kids tell me not to look at the atlas to see where we might be living.'

Graham: 'I look at some of the appointments and think they're absolutely crazy and six months later it's confirmed. I'm not saying George Burley was the wrong choice for Ipswich, not at all, but people said to me after they lost 9–0 to Man United, "Bet you're glad you didn't go there." My answer was, "Perhaps we wouldn't have lost 9–0 if I'd been there." The first thing we would have done was to get things organised. I remember John Lyall going to Newcastle and getting castigated by the Press and Kevin Keegan having a go because they played defensively. You win a lot of friends going to Old Trafford and losing 9–0. If you go there and defend and come away with a 0–0 you'll have upset Alex Ferguson and the Old Trafford crowd, but you'll be a lot happier going back on the coach than having lost 9–0.

'I had an offer around Christmas from a Cypriot side but it was at the same time the Ipswich job came up. I delayed and delayed giving them an answer, they couldn't wait any longer so they appointed a Bulgarian. But in the meantime they asked me if I would keep an eye out for English players and give them some advice on running the club. I recommended a number of players, but in the end the lack of success by English clubs in Europe, and to a certain degree the national side, turned them against English players.

'There was some good fun along the way, though, because they'd had five managers in two seasons and one of the things they asked me to do was give a report on the coach, without his knowing. I wasn't too happy with the situation but I went along and watched, or at least tried to watch. They were training under floodlights, in pouring rain, and I was watching through the bushes beside the training ground, and attempting to compile a report.

'I also had an offer from a team in Athens. I turned that down too, but it's been good experience going out there and watching the games, and I certainly wouldn't be averse to coaching abroad. The challenge of combining the talent and technique of some of the continental players with the discipline and fitness of the English game undoubtedly has its appeal. But obviously if the right offer comes up in England I would like to stay. The important thing is potential. The financial side wouldn't matter too much, the current position wouldn't, as long as I felt they had some tradition, some potential to be successful again, and you wouldn't have to breed players to sell on. That must be heart-breaking for any manager. You want to see some success in terms of winning Championships and gaining promotion and all the rest of it.

'It's an amazing situation being out of work as a manager because the situations vacant first come to notice on Ceefax. I've got a blister on my finger now from operating the remote control, to see who's got a job or out of work. I've been scouting for Derby but I've been reluctant to go to matches where the situation with the manager has been delicate. The last thing any manager wants is somebody else turning up on his doorstep, adding to the speculation, looking like a predator there, waiting to meet the right connection and get into the job.

'I've not exactly been idle. The scouting has been either for previews of teams they are due to play, or watching players. It's just for expenses only, but it keeps you in contact with the game. You never know when you are going to get back into it so you want to keep a current check on the teams and players.

'I've also served on about five transfer tribunals as representative of the League Managers' Association. We've done everything from a £5,000 transfer to Mark Draper who, I think, cost £1.25 million.

It's been interesting and surprising, a lot more complicated than I expected. The people on it have been more knowledgeable and thorough than I expected. It's more often circumstances rather than the actual talent of the player that are taken into consideration: how he's been treated by the selling club, what sort of offer has been made, what has been done to try and get him to sign a new contract. All managers moan about tribunals but the feeling among members of the committee is that if both sides are unhappy, they have done a good job. At the moment I think it's the fairest way of solving transfer disputes.'

Ann: 'It's not boring having him around. People say they dread retirement, especially men, but I've got to say it's been an absolute joy. We celebrated our silver wedding last year and he's always been in football, and I never thought I'd see the day when he'd enjoy a break so much. That's a good thing. I'm not anxious about what he's going to do because he's always come up trumps and done well. There'll be something and it could be anywhere in the world. I can see the whole family having airline tickets, not just directors' box tickets, to go and watch his team.'

Graham, though told he is on a short list of two at Notts County, is more circumspect. 'I think you look at it now cautiously. I thought Chris Nicholl did a good job at Southampton and he was out of work for three years before finally getting a chance at Walsall. I look back on what I did at Wolves and didn't think there would be any problem getting back into work quickly. You look at the situation at Notts County, because they've got the ground done, they are better than a relegation side, and you hope it will come to fruition. But you take nothing for granted now. Nothing at all.

'There's a new breed of managers. There always will be. Some have been given their chance and whether it will work out for them remains to be seen. You look at the top end and Bryan Robson's done a brilliant job at Middlesbrough, hasn't he? I think Viv Anderson found it hard going last year at Barnsley and might have learned something from that and he's gone to Middlesbrough to assist Robson. The danger for Robbo is he might think it's too easy. He's done a super job but at the other end you look at one or two who have come into it and failed miserably.'

In this dog-eat-dog world of football there is little room for sentiment and Turner was replaced at Wolves by the former

England manager, Graham Taylor. Cynics might suggest it was suitable vengeance for an old wound.

Turner says: 'I bumped into him when we were walking our dogs one Saturday morning in Sutton Park. He was with England then and planning to watch Manchester City in the afternoon. Our dog's as daft as a brush and for some reason his dog and mine started fighting, and instead of letting them get on with it he put his hand between them and one of them bit it. He always swears blind it was my dog. He finished up in hospital and with a scar down the back of his hand. He tends not to walk his dog now where I walk mine.'

For all the emotional scars inflicted by the job, 47-year-old Turner still maintains football is the life for him.

'Having been involved in it ever since leaving school at 15, I wouldn't know anything else. We talked briefly about going into the holiday business, a little hotel or something like that, but they were only brief thoughts. I can't see myself doing anything else. And you hope that next time you'll do better still. You're crazy if you don't learn from experiences, good or bad. Some of the things that perhaps went wrong at Wolves, some of the signings, you've got to try to make sure you put right at the next job.'

The Turners also have the careers of their growing offspring to concern themselves with. Three of them are in their twenties and Andrew is 15. Mark is the only one to have followed Graham into football and has the blessing of his parents.

Ann: 'I don't worry for Mark any more. You do initially because you want him to do well. It's the same as watching your husband when he's a player, but then you've got to stop yourself. You can never be a player's mum shouting from the sidelines because I don't think there's anything worse than that. We would never discourage him from making a career out of football. He had the skill there and the determination to work very, very hard and got spotted by a Wolves scout who didn't know he was the manager's son. He got there on his own.'

Graham: 'It was a difficult situation for me. Some parents think their kids can do no wrong. I think with Mark in the football club it was probably different. He had to be better than anyone else to get anything at all. It was the same in some ways when I signed Darren Ferguson from Man United. They had played at Liverpool a week earlier in a 3–3 draw after going three up. Alex said he absolutely slaughtered the players, of which Darren was one. I think he had gone on as sub. Alex felt driving home it was wrong his son was in that environment, listening to him ranting and raving, having a real fit of temper, so he decided it was better for him to go on.

'I've watched all the three lads play Sundays but I wouldn't want to go and watch Mark play now. It's up to him to make his way in the world. Alex was different, hardly missed a game at Wolves when he could go. I was up at Old Trafford for United's match against Norwich and while I was in his office Alex phoned Granada Television to see if they were taking Millwall versus Wolves live in the studio the next day. They said they were so he asked if he could go round to watch the game there.

'Mark's not done as well as we expected at Northampton but he's still only 22, he's got another year on his contract and he's got enough attributes to make a decent career out of it. He's just not put it all together yet.

'The game does involve a lot of heartache one way or another for all the family but it is worth it all. We played at Wembley in the Sherpa Van Trophy final when we were in the Fourth Division. The crowd was in excess of 80,000 and Andrew was the mascot, and whatever the heartaches and the problems, moments like that are priceless. That's why you put up with it and still want it.

'Each of them in turn, as they have been coming to their last year at school, has been my assistant scout. Andrew, over the past 12 months now, has been all over the country with me, watching games. Neil always used to do it, Mark has done it occasionally. They've had that privilege wherever they've gone, be it Liverpool, Old Trafford or any other ground, of sitting in the directors' box and you don't take that for granted. The financial rewards enable you to lead a nice lifestyle and enjoy good holidays, so it more than balances out the problems, and I still wouldn't swap it for anything.'

Notts County was one more that got away, but Ann's faith was rewarded when Graham was put in charge at third division Hereford United. Days later he was offered the job of national team coach in Egypt.